Communication policies in **Ireland**

Communication policies in Ireland

A study carried out by the
Institute of Public Administration,
An Foras Riaracháin,
and written by John Stapleton

The Unesco Press
Paris 1974

Published by, The Unesco Press,
7 Place de Fontenoy, 75700 Paris
Printed by Imprimerie Aubin, 86240 Ligugé (7678)

ISBN 92 - 3 - 101132 - 4
French edition: 92 - 3 - 201132 - 8

Preface

Communication policies are sets of principles and norms established to guide the behaviour of communication systems. They are shaped over time in the context of society's general approach to communication and to the media. Emanating from political ideologies, the social and economic conditions of the country and the values on which they are based, they strive to relate these to the real needs for and the prospective opportunities of communication.

Communication policies exist in every society, though they may sometimes be latent and disjointed, rather than clearly articulated and harmonized. They may be very general, in the nature of desirable goals and principles, or they may be more specific and practically binding. They may exist or be formulated at many levels. They may be incorporated in the constitution or legislation of a country; in over-all national policies, in the guidelines for individual administrations, in professional codes of ethics as well as in the constitutions and operational rules of particular communication institutions.

The publication of this series of studies has been undertaken as part of the programme adopted by the General Conference of Unesco at its sixteenth session, related to the analysis of communication policies as they exist at the different levels—public, institutional, professional—in selected countries. The aim of the series is to present this information in a manner which can be comparable. Thus an attempt has been made to follow, as far as possible, a fairly similar structural pattern and method of approach which was agreed between the national institutions undertaking the work.

This survey of communication policies in Ireland has been carried out by the Institute of Public Administration and written by John Stapleton. The opinions expressed by the author do not necessarily reflect the views of Unesco.

Acknowledgements

This monograph was prepared at the request of the Irish National Commission for Unesco. The Institute of Public Administration and the author wish to record their gratitude to the members and officers of the National Commission for their co-operation and guidance throughout the study.

In the absence of an academic institute in this country engaged in the full-time study of communications, an Editorial Consultative Committee, comprised of experts in the field of communications, was set up to advise on this study. The Institute of Public Administration and the author are indebted to the committee for its advice and assistance; however, the material and the views expressed in the report are the author's own.

Editorial Consultative Committee:

E. Neeson, Director, Government Information Bureau (Chairman)
M. Burns, Editor, Television News, Radio Telefís Éireann (RTE)
M. Colley, Public Relations Officer, Electricity Supply Board
J. Dunn, Director, Catholic Communications Institute
J. Eadie, National Organizer, National Union of Journalists
D. Roche, Deputy Editor, Irish Independent Newspapers
L. D. Bergin, Editor, *Nationalist and Leinster Times,* Carlow.

Contents

1 The idea of communication policy

Society has certain basic needs if it is to operate normally—needs for information, for control, for continuity of norms and values. Thus, communication is co-extensive with society: an essential condition of social living is the sharing of information and values with others. Indeed society as a whole might be viewed as a network of channels of information and institutions for communicating ideas, demands and decisions. In all but the most under-developed societies such communication will involve 'a fusion of high technology and special professionalized processes of communication with informal society-based and non-specialized processes of person to person communication'.[1][1]

In developed societies as a whole the special professionalized processes of communication—the mass media—have become highly significant institutions in that:

1. Increasingly they constitute for the majority of people one of the single more powerful means in the process through which the culture of society —its persistent habits, values and ideas—is at once transmitted and reshaped; through which the community comes to be conscious of itself and the possibilities of progress and renewal. Characteristically the mass media convey in great part the ethos of the social order in which they operate; yet at any time they also provide the means for response and potential challenge to that order.
2. In the modern State which requires of its citizens an active, continuing and informed participation in community affairs they constitute a vital component of that network of communications which are so necessary, particularly in a democracy.
3. Of their nature highly technical and specialized, the mass media, and the ancillary services to which they give rise, take up resources which constitute an important sector of the economy.
4. They seem likely, in view of their present rapid development, to prove ever more influential in the modern pattern of living.

Faced with these developments we need to examine both the values to be endorsed by our society and the role of the mass media in the attainment of its goals. Although the relationship between mass communications and

1. The figures in square brackets refer to the notes at the end of each chapter.

modern society remains in most respects problematic it seems clear that 'the effects of mass media on individuals, groups, social institutions and social relationships are highly dependent on how the media are used ar controlled'.[2] Explicit policies of communications development may ther e a need of the time. Development here means 'using, enhancing and con᾽ ᾽ng resources so as to yield new and better returns and consciously doir as by assisting the process to the desired end'.[3] Attempts to work out policy of this kind have so far been rare; certainly in democracies precede and evolutionary practice rather than design have been the norm.

Nevertheless an examination of the actions, attitudes ? assumptions of the major participants in any such venture—the State, media institutions, the professional communicators and the public—n reveal, at least implicitly, the likely elements of any such policy.

1. Lucian Pye, *Comm⋅ ⋅ and Political Development*, p. 26, Princeton University Press, 1963.
2. Denis McO⋅⋅⋅ *⋅ds a Sociology of Mass Communications*, p. 95, 96, London, Collier ᾽ ⋅td, 1969.
3. T.⋅ 'Administrative Purpose', in *Administration*, Vol. 13, No. 3, 1965,

2 The system of mass communication within the socio-economic and cultural structures of the country

2.1 Historical outline of media development

Today in Ireland, which for the purpose of this study does not include Northern Ireland, 'printing is a well established medium of mass communication serving a wide range of human activities. Despite intense and increasing competition from other media the printed word is still pre-eminent as a means of disseminating and preserving information and furthering education; and it greatly helps in carrying on most kinds of social and commercial activity'.[1]

The first printing press in Ireland became operative in 1550. The industry in its modern form was already emerging by the middle of the last century—the Dublin Typographical Provident Society was then in existence and the Dublin Master Printers Association was formed in 1899. There was a great falling off in the industry as a result of the First World War and the domestic struggle for independence from 1919 onwards. By 1926 the industry had recovered to its 1912 level; from 1932 a policy of economic protection, including duties on a wide range of imported printed matter, gave a strong stimulus to printing generally. Understandably the industry slumped again in the conditions of the Second World War; recovery was slow up to 1953, but from 1958 particularly the impact of economic development has made possible substantially sustained progress.

Printing is part of a general industry which, *in toto,* comprises the following sections: paper and paperboard manufacturing; paper products and packaging; general printing; book and magazine publishing; newspapers; and ancillary services. Not all are equally relevant to this study but it is important to be aware of 'the heterogeneous nature of the industry and the overlapping which occurs in certain sectors'.[2]

In particular the functions of printer and publisher were until recently generally combined; even today they need to be considered largely in unison. Due to the dominance of London and New York as publishing centres for the English-speaking world and the economic problems of distribution and promotion occasioned by the small scale of Irish enterprise, Irish publishing has sometimes had to operate in difficult circumstances. Its best periods have been: (a) the years of 'legislative independence' 1782–1800 when Dublin was a capital city with its own Parliament and British copyright law could be infringed with impunity; (b) the years of nationalist revival in the nineteenth century; (c) the period of the Anglo-Irish literary revival at the start of the present century.

The emergence of new publishers from 1950 onwards is however evidence of a new advance in publishing and of the sense of liveliness which pervades it.

The earliest newspapers to appear in Ireland did so in the early seventeenth century; a periodical news-sheet, *An Account of the Chief Occurrences of Ireland together with some Particulars from England,* was circulating in 1659. The first attempt at producing a commercial newspaper dates from the appearance of the *Irish Intelligencer* in 1662. Generally 'a free private enterprise press was established in Ireland parallel with its establishment in Great Britain' where 'the newspaper was the creation of the commercial middle class, mainly in the eighteenth century'.[3] These early papers in Ireland largely supported union with Britain though the *Freeman's Journal* (1763-1924) became in the nineteenth century the organ of the Home Rule Irish Parliamentary Party. *The Nation,* founded in 1842, is generally accepted as the first truly popular Irish newspaper; it is regarded as having had a considerable impact on the common people through readers who might nowadays be regarded as 'influentials' in a two-step process of communications; 'for the first time a mass means of communication was established which expressed nationalist aspirations and feelings in contemporary language . . . it helped to create the prerequisite for any successful revolutionary movement—a sympathetic climate of thought'.[4] The essential features of Irish life favouring the growth of the press from the mid nineteenth-century may well have been the increasing provision of basic literacy and education—in the English language—through the primary school system established in the 1830s and the removal of the last taxes on newspapers in 1855. Two of the existing newspapers, the *Cork Examiner* (1841) and the *Irish Times* (1859), date from this period; the *Irish Times* was the first penny newspaper in Ireland. New standards of commercial efficiency were introduced into the newspaper industry when the *Irish Daily Independent*—set up in 1891 by the minority faction of the then divided Irish Parliamentary Party to counteract the influence of the *Freeman's Journal*—became, in the hands of businessman William Martin Murphy, the *Irish Independent* (1905). The other major newspaper now published in Ireland—the *Irish Press*—is also the product of political circumstances; when groups who had opposed the treaty in arms in 1922-23 formed a constitutional party in 1926, they were confronted with a largely unsympathetic press and accordingly founded their own paper in 1931.

At about the time this urban-based press was emerging a provincial press was emerging also. The *Limerick Chronicle* was founded in 1766 and is the oldest of those currently publishing. These provincial papers were mostly weekly, based in the chief county town or city which would likely be a garrison town as well; in their editorial policy they supported, for the most part, political union with Britain. During the nineteenth century, however, as Irish constitutional nationalists moved into Westminster parliamentary politics and county and municipal government at home, many provincial newspapers were founded for the specific purpose of advocating nationalist policies. In keeping with the popular mood many of them made the transition to support for Sinn Fein from 1917 onwards and shared the harassment, often amounting to closure, that had previously been the lot of advanced nationalist periodicals. By 1870 there were 103 local/provincial weeklies in the area of the country under discussion, working to a circulation survival minimum of 1,500. Nineteen of these survive to number 'more than a third of the provincial weeklies of today (1969) . . . proof of their durability in widely varying conditions'.[5] Although less than half of the number of papers published in 1870 are produced today, they account for a circulation about four times as great.

The first film exhibition in Ireland was given in Dublin in November 1896 by the Lumière company of Paris only a year after they had pioneered the development of the cinema. By 1909 the new medium was sufficiently established to warrant the opening of a full-time cinema: the Volta in Mary Street, Dublin. Its first manager for a brief period, 1909–10, was James Joyce. From that beginning the cinema industry in Ireland—as distinct from the film industry—enjoyed virtually unbroken expansion down to the end of the 1950s. It was sufficiently well established by the end of the First World War to sustain film rental companies. By 1934 there were 194 cinemas attracting 18 million visits annually; by 1945 it was one of the main national means of entertainment, and audiences continued to expand until they reached their peak around 1957.

As if to match this early interest, the history of film-making in Ireland goes back to the early days of the cinematographic art. Local news-reels were on exhibition at the turn of the century. Between 1910 and 1914 Sidney Olcott made a series of films on Irish subjects. In 1917 two Irish companies entered the film business: the Film Company in Ireland, composed mainly of Abbey Theatre actors, which had limited success with feature films, and General Film Supply who dealt in news-reels, animated cartoons and commercial publicity shots. However film production in Ireland remained largely the work of visiting foreign companies, particularly when the introduction of sound film (1928) substantially increased the capital required to undertake the making of feature films. Despite the setting-up, with substantial State aid, of Ardmore Studios by a private enterprise group in 1958 and the incorporation of the Irish Film Finance Company Ltd (a State-sponsored body) in 1960, domestic feature-film production is negligible. Two feature documentaries *Mise Eire* and *Saoirse ?* incorporating film of great historical importance from the beginning of the century onwards were produced by the Irish language organization—Gael Linn—in 1959 and 1961. In 1956 the same organization started to issue monthly and later fortnightly shorts. In 1959 this enterprise became a weekly news-reel which continued in the sixties when the coming of television brought about the end of the cinema news-reel in most countries. On the other hand 'short film production . . . has now reached a volume large enough to constitute a minor film industry and keep a body of professional film-makers at work in Ireland; . . . the list of international honours won by Irish shorts in recent years testifies to the standard already achieved and the potential of Irish films'. Over-all, however, the Film Industry Committee (1968) concluded that 'many recommendations, proposals and suggestions from various quarters over a large number of years . . . did not result in the establishment of an Irish film industry'.[6]

A national sound-broadcasting service was established by the Wireless Telegraphy Act 1926. The first moves were made as early as 1923 with the publication of a government White Paper on the subject. At that time the government was faced with the basic task of reconstruction following the war of independence and the subsequent civil war. But it was in this fundamental context that the new service was viewed; it was to denote 'a separate existence . . . not only political but also social and cultural'.[7] Not surprisingly in the circumstances—and given the centralizing tendency of the new State— it was decided that broadcasting should be run by the State within a government department as a public service, though with provision for raising revenue by advertising. The staff were civil servants. In 1953—after the station had undergone two major expansions in 1933 and 1947—Comhairle Radio Éireann was set up: 'a small advisory council to run Radio Éireann in practice while the Minister retained overriding authority'; within the doctrine of ministerial responsibility it made Radio Éireann 'as nearly independent as possible'[8] and marked the first step towards giving broadcasting a status of its own. The process culminated in the Broadcasting Authority Act 1960 which established as a statutory corporation, independent for the most part of the government, employing its own staff, a joint authority for radio and the new television service: Radio Éireann, later Radio Telefís Éireann.

Questions about the possible introduction of a television service had been asked in the Dail (House of Representatives) as far back as 1938. Public demand for the service grew continuously after the BBC opened a regional station in Northern Ireland. In March 1958, when there were some 30,000 television receivers in the country availing of British transmissions, a commission was established to report on the practicability of establishing a television service. The commission reported within terms of reference which required that the television system must be subject to the effective control of an Irish public authority but did not provide for the direct operation of the service by that body. Ultimately, however, the government decided that the new authority should have direct responsibility for all aspects of the service, including programme output. Irish television went on the air for the first time on 31 December 1961.

2.2 The socio-political structure and system of mass communication

Ireland, in virtue of Article 5 of its Constitution, is 'a sovereign, independent, democratic state' with effective jurisdiction over twenty-six of the thirty-two counties of the island. The State has been established as a representative constitutional democracy in which 'in the minds of the people . . . fundamental rights such as freedom of speech, assembly and religion, the rule of law . . . are now to be regarded as virtually unalterable'.[9] The use of this democratic independence 'to develop its own life, political, economic and cultural, in accordance with its own genius and traditions' (Article 1 of the Constitution) represents the most fundamental commitment in the Irish political culture.

In terms of institutional forms and conduct the political culture is also heavily influenced by the experience under the Union (with Great Britain, 1801–1922). This influence continues because, for example, of geographical proximity, heavy reliance on the British market for external trading and the considerable penetration of Irish society by the British mass media.

Basic data on the socio-political structure and system of mass communication will be found in the Appendixes. The salient features of the situation are that the total population and population density are among the lowest in Europe, but the significant decline in heavy annual emigration, earlier marriages and greater longevity have combined to produce for the first time since the State was founded a sustained upward curve in population figures. However the dependency ratio is still among the highest in Europe. This results in high unit capital and distributive costs in the provision of services, including of course communications facilities. The combination of small population and a *per capita* income that is relatively low by West European standards limits in absolute terms the scale of media operation, though in the Irish context they may be quite large: Independent Newspapers Ltd and Irish Cinemas Ltd were among the fifty largest industrial companies in 1972. The dominance of London as a communications centre for the English-speaking world limits Irish media export potential and impinges on their already restricted domestic market. Reception of BBC radio is general and as many as three channels of British television can be received in the eastern (most populous) part of the country. British newspapers have a significant circulation; the provision of inexpensive paperback literature and much of the market for periodicals is in British and American hands. However a decade of economic growth has benefited Irish publishing; in particular there has been a growth in the number of technical and professional publications reflecting the increased sophistication of the Irish economy. There has always been a well-developed religious press.

As late as 1966 a slight majority of the population resided in rural communities of fewer than 1,500 inhabitants; in 1969 agriculture still rivalled industry as a source of employment though not in output as a proportion of GNP. Urbanization is a major social trend but is not evenly distributed: Dublin contains almost 30 per cent of the population and continues to expand; altogether 50 per cent live in the eastern province of Leinster of which Dublin is the centre. There are only three other cities of over 30,000 population, consequently in Ireland smaller towns fulfil the functions performed by 50,000–150,000 sized towns in Europe. Few (even of the towns) have a wide range of social facilities; an exception perhaps might be made in the case of the cinema; in 1966 there were seventy-one cinemas serving populations

15

of less than 2,000. Incomes in the Dublin/Leinster area are substantially higher than those of the west; Dublin is not only the administrative capital; it is also the social, commercial and industrial capital of the country. These influences are reflected in the pattern of media output and usage: 'the communications media too are overwhelmingly Dublin based and can with some justification be said to have an urban cultural orientation'.[10] The outstanding exception—apart from Radio na Gaeltachta, the Irish language broadcasting station, and the Cork Examiner newspaper company—is the provincial weekly press based largely on the county, an administrative and cultural unit 'powerfully supported by local sentiment and tradition'.[11] A problem which confronts the provincial newspapers, however, is the shift in population towards Dublin and other big centres. The decline in population in the western areas mainly has affected circulations of both national and provincial newspapers but, whereas national papers can usually recoup these readers from other areas, this is not case with the local papers.

Between the central and local—county and municipal—government there are no defined territorial units of administration which might serve as focal points for middle range media development; though there is a growing tendency to regionalize services on a functional basis which may ultimately become comprehensive. Within the structure of central government there exists however the institution of the 'State-sponsored body': public enterprises, free from detailed ministerial control, set up to provide services which because of their scale and/or social importance are not left to private enterprise. Since 1960 this has been the institutional form of the radio and television services. Since April 1972 a special radio service—Radio na Gaeltachta—has been provided for the Gaeltacht (native Irish-speaking areas). The existence of these communities and the bilingual status of the State, with the Irish language as 'the first official language' (Article 8 of the Constitution) sustains an Irish-language influence or sector across the entire range of mass media operations.

REFERENCES

1. Committee on Industrial Organisation, *Report on Survey of the Printing Industry*, p. 26, Dublin, Stationery Office, 1963.
2. Committee on Industrial Progress, *Report on Paper, Paper Products, Printing and Publishing Industry*, p. 6, Dublin, Stationery Office, 1970.
3. Basil Chubb, *The Government and Politics of Ireland*, p. 123, Stanford University Press, 1970; Raymond Williams, *The Long Revolution*, p. 197, London, Pelican, 1965.
4. Speech of the then Prime Minister, Mr Jack Lynch, T. D., to the World Congress of the International Federation of Journalists, 29 April 1968.
5. Daniel Nolan, *The Provincial Press in the Changing Economy*, p. 19, Tralee, The Kerryman Ltd. (Private circulation.)
6. *Report of the Film Industry Committee*, p. 9, 24 and 25, Dublin, Stationery Office, 1968.

7. Maurice Gorham, quoting Postmaster-General J. J. Walsh (1924), in *Forty Years of Irish Broadcasting,* p. 12, Dublin, The Talbot Press, 1967.

8. ibid, p. 208.

9. *Report of the Committee on the Constitution,* p. 4, Dublin, Stationery Office, 1967.

10. Christina Murphy, 'Some Urban/Rural Problems in Ireland', *Education for Europe* (Geneva), Vol. 4, December 1971, p. 24–30.

11. *Local Government Reorganisation,* p. 25, Dublin, Stationery Office, 1971.

17

2

3 Public policy

3.1 The constitutional context

No overt and fully comprehensive public policy has been formulated in respect of mass communications in Ireland. Implicitly, however, the dominant influence at all levels of policy-making has been the 'social responsibility' model[1] of communications behaviour. Basically this model seeks to reconcile freedom of the mass media with responsibility to the community and the ideal of public service; it is well adapted to the culture outlined in the previous chapter in which basic liberal democratic freedoms operate in conjunction with a socially pervasive conception of the common good.

This position is depicted in Article 40.6.1 of the Constitution:

The State guarantees liberty for the exercise of the following rights subject to public order and morality:

The right of the citizens to express freely their convictions and opinions.

The education of public opinion being however a matter of such grave import to the common good the State shall endeavour to ensure that the organs of public opinion, such as the radio, the press, the cinema, while preserving their rightful liberty of expression, including criticism of Government policy, shall not be used to undermine public order or morality or the authority of the State. The publication or utterance of blasphemous, seditious or indecent matter is an offence which shall be punishable in accordance with law.

The guarantee of free expression in the Irish Constitution is therefore explicit and, since enactment of the Constitution, has never arisen for judicial consideration at the level of the Supreme Court. It is, in the terms of the Constitution itself, a 'personal right' from which freedom of the press is inferred and derived. Certain limitations in the article apply expressly to 'the organs of public opinion'; and the provision 'subject to public order and morality' is constitutional legitimacy for the censorship of films and censorship of publications legislation discussed below.

3.2 The official information structures

'In a democracy the importance of informing is as great as the importance of being informed. Public representatives and public bodies acting as they

18

do on behalf of the entire community have an especial role to play in keeping the public adequately informed'.[2]

In Ireland, the State has a number of specialized agencies for disseminating information:

1. The Government Publications Sale Office, since 1930 an integral part of the Stationery Office. The office is responsible, *inter alia,* 'for the printing, publication, distribution and sale of Government publications, is an agent for the sale of publications of certain international bodies and undertakes certain agency work for government departments and some state-sponsored bodies'.

2. The chief central information agency, the government information bureau, was set up in 1934. The bureau issues statements on behalf of the government and departments of State; arranges interviews with ministers and senior departmental officers; deals with queries from the public and the public media, briefs journalists from at home and abroad and arranges press conferences on behalf of government departments; collaborates in radio and television programmes relating to aspects of government policy and administration and advises and co-ordinates on aspects of departmental information and publicity campaigns. A process of reorganization and expansion of the bureau was undertaken in 1968 and is continuing. Since April 1972 the bureau has published *Eolas,* a monthly information bulletin which aims 'to provide a digest of current information on the activities of government departments and agencies'.

3. Every department has a nominated officer who handles communications with the bureau. Increasingly the individual departments have their own information officers who handle specifically departmental matters directly with the media.

4. The Department of Foreign Affairs has particular responsibilities in the area of external publicity; it contains information and cultural relations sections. In view of the interest of other departments in this work it operates an Interdepartmental Advisory Committee on Publicity Abroad. The department publishes, on average monthly, a bulletin entitled *Eire/Ireland.*

5. To promote the supply of information about Ireland in an international context The Irish News Agency was established as a limited company in 1949 to engage 'in the collection, dissemination, distribution and publication of news and intelligence inside and outside the State'. It closed in 1957. In November 1971 the government engaged an international agency, on a contractual basis, to help to bring better understanding abroad to contemporary Irish affairs.

3.3 The press

'The role of a free press in preserving the democratic process is a very important one, so important indeed that it is impossible to visualize the survival of the democratic system without it'.[3]

A Council of Europe symposium (Salzburg, 1968) on human rights and mass communication distinguished between those countries which have a 'press law' regulating in detail matters relating to the press, and those which have a 'law of the press' whereby 'no specific privileges are accorded to the press . . . freedom consists in the right to print without previous licence subject to the operation of the ordinary law'.[4] Freedom of the press in Ireland is of this latter kind.

In this context the legal provisions which impinge most upon the press tend to concern the following four areas:

Control in the interests of public safety and State authority. This involves chiefly the provisions of the Official Secrets Act (1963) and the Offences Against the State Acts (1939–72). The potentially severe restrictions in these Acts are not being invoked against the press; for instance, they have not been invoked throughout the present Northern Ireland crisis despite the actions taken in respect of the State-sponsored broadcasting services (see Section 3.6, below). During the Second World War an official and strict censorship was operated under special legislation so as to avoid endangering Ireland's neutrality.

Control in the interest of judicial authority: The law here relates mainly to criminal procedure and pre-trial publicity; the limits of fair comment; and contempt of court. A recent case of a journalist in contempt of court is dealt with in Chapter 5.

Control in the interests of private reputations: Essentially this involves provisions relating to libel in statute and common law. This as a particularly difficult area for the press as, at the margin, the law is not easy to interpret. A recent innovation in this area has produced problems of changed practice for the newspapers and has resulted in some of them occasionally being in breach of the law. Since the Criminal Procedure Act (1967) it has been an offence to publish evidence of preliminary hearings of indictable offences (other than the basic facts that such proceedings took place) unless, at the request of the accused, permission to do so is granted by the judge. The press may *not* however be excluded from the hearings.

Control in the interests of public morality: In practice this largely involves Part III and Part IV of the Censorship of Publications (1922) Act. Part III of that Act makes it an offence 'to print or publish . . . in relation to any judicial proceedings for divorce, nullity of marriage, judicial separation or restitution of conjugal rights . . .' any material other than certain specified particulars, for breach of which the national newspapers were fined heavily in 1971. Part IV of the Act prohibits the publication of material 'which advocates or which might reasonably be supposed to advocate the unnatural prevention of conception or the procurement of abortion or miscarriage . . .'; but it is not enforced, at least in respect of news papers.

The important social and other roles which the press fulfils cannot be divorced from the economics of the newspaper industry. National economic policy in the past decade has emphasized the objective of free trade;

and the impact of free trade on the printing industries generally has been a major worry during that time. Reports on the industries were commissioned from the Committee on Industrial Organization (CIO) in 1962–64 and its successor the Committee on Industrial Progress (CIP) in 1970. The CIO report noted that the complete abolition of the present tariffs on printed material would involve a loss of about 10 per cent of the total home market. Both reports stressed the need for rationalization and modernization; the CIP report noted numerous ways in which public policy might assist the newspaper sector particularly. These included:

1. The provision of adaptation grants to facilitate modernization and re-equipment; this recommendation has been endorsed in respect of the provincial press and is being considered in the case of the national newspapers.

2. A lessening in the impact of taxation which 'had seriously eroded profits and . . . was a serious impediment to the building up of reserves'.[5] In 1963 a direct sales 'turnover tax' was introduced from which the newspapers were not exempt; by 1970 wholesale and turnover taxes combined stood at the rate of 16 per cent. Four-fifths of this tax was absorbed by the industry itself; taken in conjunction with corporate taxation this placed a major burden on the press over-all. An intensive lobby against taxation of newspapers has had partial success in that the rate of value-added tax (VAT) to apply to newspapers, from November 1972, will at 5.26 per cent be much less than the wholesale and turnover taxes it replaces. However, advertising expenditure now becomes liable to VAT and there are fears that this may affect press revenue from this source. On the whole the press would prefer taxation relief, as an aid to re-equipment, rather than the proposals for adaptation grants mentioned above. Generally newspaper profits showed a recovery in 1972/73.

3. A reduction in the rate of freight and postal charges; while preferential rates apply to printed matter these compare rather unfavourably in certain details with those elsewhere. However, the Department of Posts and Telegraphs takes the view that the postal services should pay for themselves and further concessions to users of the printed paper post rate would aggravate the position and involve loss of revenue.

4. Some machinery to guard against the possibility of foreign take-overs of existing daily newspapers which 'could have far reaching implications . . . [requiring] careful consideration'.[6] In February 1973, when it was rumoured that a take-over offer was being made for the Independent Group of Newspapers, the Minister for Industry and Commerce stated that 'a situation in which ownership or control of Irish newspapers passed into non-Irish hands would be unacceptable'.[7]

5. The CIO had already approved the fact that newsprint is in general imported free of both protective and revenue duties; and this provision has been safeguarded in negotiations for EEC entry. (Finland, Canada and Sweden account for most of the newsprint supply.) Home production

of newsprint meets only a relatively small part of demand. Another CIO report had envisaged as 'a factor of prime importance in regard to the future of this industry . . . the setting up of pulp mills to produce chemical and semi-chemical pulps from native timber . . . [which] would involve substantial capital investment'. The CIP report, however, termed this 'unrealistic . . . in the foreseeable future'.[8]

6. Finally CIP noted the dependence of newspaper revenue—particularly advertising revenue—on the state of the economy.

Within the legal and constitutional framework, relations between the public policy-makers and the press are largely a matter of prevailing attitudes which reflect the tensions that from time to time characterize government-press relationships in most democracies. Thus the conviction of some newspaper publishers for breach of Part III of the Censorship of Publications Act; the concern of the all-party Committee on the Constitution—set up in 1966 to review the constitutional, legislative and institutional bases of government—with parliamentary privilege and 'improper press comment'; and the section of the Prohibition of Forcible Entry and Occupation Act which made it an offence to 'encourage or advocate' any actions already embodied as offences in the Act, each met with varying degrees of press opposition.

The nature of the relationship between government and press was remarked on by the Prime Minister *(Taoiseach)* in a speech to the World Congress of the International Federation of Journalists in Dublin (1968). He thought 'the ideal relationship . . . ought to be one of responsible partnership each upholding the just rights and legitimate functions of the other' while recognizing that 'if freedom is to be preserved governments and press in their own vital interests must, so to speak, keep their distance'.[9]

3.4 Publishing

Publishing activity in Ireland expanded substantially in the late 1960s. A number of factors contributed to this growth; most significant, in the view of CIP, have been the expansion in the number of post-primary and higher education students (particularly since 1967) and the relaxation of the censorship laws in the same year.

A system of post-publication preventive censorship has existed in respect of books and periodicals since a Censorship of Publications Board was established by statute in 1929. By an amending Act of 1946 an Appeal Board was also established. The system involves a departure from the prosecution method inherited from the British as 'clumsy, wasteful and ineffective due to the fact that most publishers were outside the jurisdiction of the courts'[10]; and in fact the bulk of submitted material reaches the censors through customs officials rather than from individual members of the public. The chief grounds of prohibition of display or sale are that a work: (a) is 'in its general tendency indecent or obscene', where obscene is to be 'construed as including suggestive of or inciting to sexual immorality or unnatural vice or likely in any other similar way to corrupt or deprave'; (b) 'advocates the unnatural prevention of conception or the procurement of abortion or miscarriage'; (c) 'in the case of periodicals they devote an unduly large proportion of space to the publication of matter relating to crime'.

The operation of the censorship system has been until recently one of the more persistent sources of controversy in Irish life; though it ought to be said that the grounds of prohibition have never extended to questions of a political or economic kind. The censorship Acts themselves have been described as workmanlike measures but their implementation is considered to have been, at times, unnecessarily strict. Significantly the initial (1957–58) liberalization involved an administrative measure—the Minister for Justice reconstituted the Board; a liberalizing Act of 1967 formalized the new policy. This made it possible to remove the prohibition order on a book after twelve years; the result was the release of over 5,000 of the 10,000 titles that had accumulated on the Register of Prohibited Publications. Provision exists in the Act for rebanning a released book but such occurrences have been rare. Finally the Act lifted the twelve-month time-limit on representations to the Appeal Board against a ban.

A problem in the operation of the censorship system has been posed by the advent of the paperback: one viewpoint is that 'the censorship board very often "misses" paperbacks . . . because they sell very fast and by the time a ban is announced average sales have been achieved . . . [there is] little doubt that the standard of paperbacked books in Dublin shops has deteriorated in recent years'.[11]

The effect of the changes in censorship on Irish publishing has largely been indirect—the main target of the system has generally been the cheap import—in that it reflects and encourages new social and cultural attitudes which seem likely to benefit publishing. A similar effect is expected from the budgetary exemption from income tax accorded to authors of 'works of cultural merit'; although this is a personal concession and not a corporate exemption of the publishing company the indirect effects on Irish publishing ought to be beneficial. More directly the State has been assisting publishers' exports. CIP had noted that export figures, while unreliable, were not very flattering to the Irish printing and publishing industry; since then Coras Trachtala Teo. (the Export Board) has assisted publishers' displays in Frankfurt, New York and New Delhi. The Cultural Relations Committee of the Department of Foreign Affairs also commissions works to serve as cultural ambassadors abroad. However publishers fault public policy in a number of respects: they too would like further concessions on postal and freight charges; they seek complete product exemption from taxation which is resented as 'virtually unknown in most other countries . . . [is] not only a tax on knowledge but contrary to the spirit of the Unesco charter'. [12]

Book-buying might be viewed as the outcome of growing affluence and extensive educational opportunity both of which are relatively recent in Ireland. In these circumstances a valuable contribution of public policy towards catering for and fostering reading interests has been the public library service operated by county and municipal authorities under the general supervision of the Department of Local Government. Although enabling legislation had existed since 1855 the modern and effective origins of the service date from the Local Government Act 1925. The Public Libraries Act 1947 established the Library Council 'generally to promote library interests including the improvement of the public library service'. Reports of the Council indicating that inadequate financial provision more than any other single factor had retarded development encouraged the department to make available (1961) capital grants in respect of buildings, vehicles and book stock, with the result that the public library is now taking a more important place in the life of the community. Much however remains to be done; low *per capita* current expenditure reflects a continuing low priority for libraries among the local authorities. The interim report of the National Adult Education Survey[13] termed the libraries 'an essential educational service to the community' and argued that 'possibly a more effective use could be made of them . . . if responsibility for their operation were transferred . . . to the Department of Education'; or perhaps, as the Devlin Report suggested, to a proposed Department of National Culture. Within the central administration too, much remains to be done. There is a need for 'an overall development plan based on known and estimated needs . . . one which commits all libraries to the public service . . . the finances for this service must be made available as a valuable national investment and as the essential corollary to investment in education'.[14] The future development of the National Library has been the subject of a study by Dr K. W. Humphreys, Librarian, Birmingham University, who was appointed as consultant in 1969. The recommendations of his report, presented in 1971, are under consideration.

3.5 Cinema and film industry

In addition to the ordinary provisions of common and statute law as it affects trade in general, the cinema trade—involving film producers, distributors and exhibitors—is subject to certain special Acts affecting the exhibitors. The Cinematograph Act 1909 requires that all cinemas be licensed by the local authority in order to ensure minimum safety standards. A duty operates on imported films but entertainment tax, levied on box-office receipts, was abolished in 1962. The most important legislation, however, is the Censorship of Films Acts 1923–70 which in many respects parallel the censorship of publications provisions. The founding Act established an Official Censor of Films and a Censorship of Films Appeal Board. 'No picture shall be exhibited in public . . . unless and until the censor has certified that the whole of such picture is fit for exhibition in public'; a certificate may be refused or granted 'subject to such restrictions and conditions . . . as in the opinion of the Official Censor are necessary'; these may involve deletions from the film or limitations on time or place of exhibition or composition of the audience. The grounds of prohibition are that 'such picture or some part thereof is unfit for general exhibition in public by reason of its being indecent, obscene or blasphemous or because the exhibition thereof in public would tend to inculcate principles contrary to public morality or would be otherwise subversive of public morality'.

As with censorship of publications, dissatisfaction with the operation rather than the principles of the system was allayed through the reconstruction of the Appeal Board in 1964; in 1970 an amending Act made it possible for films banned prior to 1965 to be resubmitted to the censor, and made general provision for right of review of banned films after seven years. This trend seems likely to be continued under the new censor appointed in June 1972 who has been actively concerned with motion pictures and has also worked in public relations.

The censorship of films legislation differs from that of censorship of publications in a number of respects. Among these are the provision of a single official censor rather than a censorship board; the absence of any 'general tendency' phrase qualifying 'indecent or obscene'; and the absence of annual reports conveying official information on the functioning of the system.

Long-discussed proposals for the establishment of a native film industry have not yet come to fruition. In November 1967, however, the Minister for Industry and Commerce appointed the Film Industry Committee 'to examine the problems involved in the establishment of an Irish film industry and to advise on how they could be solved'. The committee reported that the difficulties in the way of the establishment of an Irish film industry are formidable but the benefits likely to accrue are sufficient to warrant the effort.

The benefits the committee envisaged include: (a) the development and employment of Irish creative, artistic and technical skills; (b) the opportunity for Irish cinema audiences to see themselves and their way of life reflected on the screen; (c) the projection abroad of a true image of Ireland and the Irish way of life and traditions.

The committee was conscious of the tension between the commercial and cultural considerations involved in establishing a film industry; it was 'right that any proposals for the establishment of an Irish film industry should be measured against these criteria [for assisting industrial promotion generally] but we realized that our task involved more than this measurement . . . the cinema is among the most powerful communications media of the age exerting as it does a deep influence on the habits, attitudes, motivations and aspirations of its audiences . . . a dearth of native material is not conducive to a sense of community awareness and identity'.[15] Specifically, the committee recommended that feature-film production and short-film production be distinguished; an Irish feature film it defined as one made in

Ireland with a significant Irish creative, artistic and technical content; such films should be able to justify themselves commercially which in the case of short films would not be the major consideration. Furthermore it identified two categories of feature films: those in the £200,000 range in which financial assistance would be limited to pre-production costs and those in the £50,000 range requiring substantial financial assistance. It recommended that a Film Board should be established to give initial and continuing effect to the committee's proposals; it should not itself engage in the production of films; its role should be 'the creation of conditions in which other interests will be likely to do this and the stimulating of these interests to undertake the task'.[16] The board should, however, directly involve itself in securing distribution agreements, co-production agreements, the provision of training and production facilities, the tendering of advice on public policy and the establishment of a national film archive. It should also promote the planned increase of short-film production and encourage the production of television commercials in this country.

The recommendations of the committee have been incorporated in the Film Industry Bill (1970) which has received a first reading in the Dail.

3.6 Radio and television

Radio Telefís Éireann (RTE) is the national broadcasting authority, charged under the Broadcasting Authority Act 1960 to 'establish and maintain a national television and sound broadcasting service' and endowed with 'all such powers as are necessary or incidental to that purpose'. Institutionally it takes the form of a State-sponsored body and reports annually to the Minister for Posts and Telegraphs, who has administrative responsibility for broadcasting. Subject to certain powers reserved to the minister, the authority enjoys 'a large measure of freedom in ordering its own affairs'.[17]

Broadcasting has been thought of for over forty years as something done by a single public body; and the 1960 Act conferred a monopoly of broadcasting on the authority. The monopoly, however, only relates to broadcasts originating within the State. As already indicated, British services are widely available; the latest extension of this influence dates from March 1970 when public pressure resulted in a government decision to allow up to 500 connexions per aerial in the wired distribution of external television services where these are available off air. Pressure for the extension of multi-channel services to the country at large have been resisted on the grounds of breach of international copyright regulations, the cost of micro-wave links required to effect it and the likely impact of any such move on the audience sizes and finances of RTE. In March 1973 the Broadcasting Review Committee in an interim report recommended the establishment of a second television channel, under the control of the RTE authority, as a step towards the provision of choice in the present single-channel areas.

It is estimated that it would take between two and three years from the date of Government approval to establish this service. The Broadcasting Review Committee had been set up in 1971 'to review the progress of the television and sound broadcasting services since the enactment of the Broadcasting Authority Act 1960 with particular reference to the objectives prescribed in that Act, and to make any recommendations considered appropriate in regard to the further development of the services'. Under the Broadcasting (Offences) Act 1968 the government has taken powers to deal with pirate broadcasting 'from ships, aircraft and certain marine structures'. RTE's financial responsibilities are 'to meet all sums properly chargeable to current account and to make suitable provision with respect to capital expenditure'. As to capital, RTE has to date been financed—apart from an initial transfer of assets and a capital grant—by repayable government advances up to a permitted maximum of £3 million and surpluses earned on the operating account; under the 1960 Act it is entitled to borrow from external sources under certain conditions and has done so on a limited scale. As to current revenue, it receives the net receipts of licence fees, fixed by the Minister for Posts and Telegraphs and collected by his department, and revenue raised from advertising. The extent of advertising time, as of broadcasting hours generally, is fixed by the authority 'subject to the approval of the Minister'.

The authority consists of between seven and nine members, including a chairman. It is appointed, subject to a maximum five-year period of office with eligibility of members for re-appointment, 'on such terms as the Government may determine from time to time'; the terms of appointment must, however, be laid before both houses of the Oireachtas (Parliament). The chief executive officer, the Director-General, is appointed by the authority with the approval of the minister. A member of the authority may 'at any time' resign or be removed from office by the government. The power of removal was used for the first time in November 1972 in circumstances outlined later in this section. Two chairmen of the authority have in fact resigned; the first in 1966 on policy grounds—he thought the station was going 'too far too fast'[18]—the other in 1970 when his son became a junior minister in the government.

The legal monopoly of broadcasting enjoyed by RTE, and its status as a State-sponsored body, involves the imposition on it of some limitations and responsibilities additional to those impinging on the press.

Section 17 of the Broadcasting Authority Act requires the authority 'to bear constantly in mind the national aims of restoring the Irish language and preserving and developing the national culture'. This has always been a major emphasis in broadcasting policy and has found renewed expression recently in the establishment of Radio na Gaeltachta. This emphasis too is apparent in the Devlin Report which, proposing the allocation of responsibilities to departments on a functional basis, recommended that RTE report to an envisaged Department of National Culture rather than to a newly constituted Department of Transport and Communications (incorporating the present Department of Posts and Telegraphs).

Section 18 of the Act requires the authority to ensure that information, news and features are 'presented objectively and impartially and without any expression of the authority's own view'. The authority is prohibited from accepting any advertisement which is directed towards any religious or political end or has any relation to an industrial dispute. The interpretation of what constitutes objectivity and impartiality in news and features has inevitably been a source of sporadic public controversy. A serious dispute arose out of a television programme on illegal money-lending in Dublin in November 1969; claims advanced in the programme were rejected in the Dail by the Minister for Justice but the programme was endorsed by the authority. As a result a judicial tribunal was established to consider, *inter alia,* 'the authenticity of the programme'; the tribunal, although it commended the desire to bring public attention to a serious social problem was, on balance, critical of the programme. The authority 'took careful account of the criticisms in the report . . . and as a consequence reviewed the working procedures for current affairs television programmes'.[19]

Finally, under section 31 of the Act, the authority is obliged, on receipt of a written directive from the Minister for Posts and Telegraphs, 'to allocate broadcasting time for any announcement by or on behalf of any Minister of State' in connexion with the functions of his office; similary 'the Minister may direct the Authority in writing to refrain from broadcasting any particular matter or matter of any particular class'. The latter provision has been invoked once: on 1 October 1971 the minister directed the RTE authority 'to refrain from broadcasting any matter of the following class i.e. any matter that could be calculated to promote the aims or activities of any organization which engages in, promotes, encourages or advocates the obtaining of any particular objective by violent means'. In a statement issued on the following day the authority stated that it did not believe that it had helped to promote the aims and activities of any organization of the type referred to in the direction; and the authority drew attention to the difficulties of observing a direction couched in such 'general terms'. In September 1972 the Director-General of RTE stated that 'the Ministers statutory directive is being implemented by RTE while meeting its basic broadcasting responsibility to comprehensive and authentic reporting.[20]

On 21 November 1972 the minister informed the RTE authority that a broadcast made by RTE two days earlier was in contravention of the ministerial direction and asked what action the authority proposed to take. In its reply of 23 November, the authority set out the difficulties it had in implementing the direction and the steps it had taken in its attempt to comply with it. It asserted that the handling of the programme material in question was on the same lines as in previous programmes which had not been questioned; but it admitted that the editorial decisions taken in this particular instance showed defective judgement in the context of the direction and outlined new institutional procedures to safeguard against any recurrence. The government's view was that the direction was 'clear and precise' and it regarded this response as inadequate—on 24 November 1972, it dismissed the members of the authority *in toto* and appointed a new authority to hold office until May 1973.

Beyond the formal provisions of the 1960 Act there are of course the informal pressures—actual or alleged—which have, as would be expected in a democracy, provided a staple of political conflict particularly in the decade of television. A member of the Dail—a political scientist and a former television interviewer and commentator—has observed 'an essential contradiction between the nature of party politics and the role of communication medium, especially in a monopolistic situation'.[21] In the view of a former Prime Minister: 'Radio Telefís Éireann was set up by legislation as an instrument of public policy and as such is responsible to the Government. The Government has overall responsibility for its conduct and especially the obligation to ensure that its programmes do not offend against the public interest . . . to this extent the Government reject the view that Radio Telefís Éireann should be, either generally or in regard to its current affairs and news programmes, completely independent of Government supervision'.[22]

On the other hand, in a history of Irish broadcasting, it was noted that 'it took some time for members of the Dail to realize that the Minister was no longer legally responsible for everything that went out over the air. Even when they ceased putting down questions, except those relating to the Minister's reserved powers, they asserted their right to treat the debate on the Posts and Telegraphs Estimate as an occasion to give their views on such programmes as they had seen or heard'.[23] The problem is particularly acute in the case of television since, because it is so recent 'there is the absence of any settled expectations about their behaviour towards each other'[24] among politicians and communicators. Despite these problems, however, RTE has, over the first decade of its existence, achieved considerable operational freedom.

3.7 The Irish language and the mass media

Article 8.1 of the Constitution states that 'the Irish language as the national language is the first official language'; the official policy towards Irish is its restoration 'as a general medium of communication'.[25] In the view of the Commission on the Restoration of Irish, 1958–63, 'the most the educational system can achieve. . . is to give each generation . . . an oral mastery of the language; . . . command of the language will be lost . . . unless they come into constant contact with it afterwards'. In this respect the Commission noted that 'our very geographical position leaves us particularly susceptible to all the modern media of mass communication of the English speaking world', and stressed the importance of the use of Irish in 'the media of culture and entertainment'.[26]

A State body for publishing in Irish, An Gum, set up in 1926 became the most extensive publisher of Irish books; since 1952 financial aid has been available for the publication of works in Irish by commercial publishers. Some periodicals too are in receipt of State aid which has undoubtedly helped them to survive and in some cases to expand considerably. Generally the language commission felt 'that the tremendous amount of publication which the language requires . . . will never be provided under the existing system'; it recommended 'a Publications Board . . . enjoying considerable independence and liberally endowed with funds . . . to cover all aspects of publishing in Irish'.[27] The government did not accept the necessity to establish a special State Board but it did agree to reorganize, co-ordinate and expand progressively the activities of existing bodies, to give them greater freedom of action and to establish an Advisory Board.

Apart from a few short films produced by the National Film Institute and individual government departments, all existing films in Irish have been made by Gael Linn which has recently commenced production of colour documentaries. Gael Linn receives a small annual grant for the purpose of film-making but, in the view of the Language Commission, this is not sufficient. The policy of the Irish Film Finance Corporation has been to grant loans only in the case of those films which may reasonably be expected to turn out financially profitable; hence no films in Irish have been financed from this source. The Film Industry Committee stated that 'if Irish is to be seen to be relevant to present day living it is essential that the cinema, with its very considerable influence and aura of modernity, should have a part to play in the restoration of the language by frequent presentation of films in Irish';[28] it recommended that short film production in Irish should be considerably extended. Earlier the Language Commission had requested that 200 short films per annum as well as an occasional feature-length film of high artistic and technical merit should be produced in Irish; it suggested a small tax on film distributors as a guaranteed source of revenue for the project. The tax proposal was rejected by the government (and the Film Industry Committee) but a more extensive grants scheme towards the production of short films has been promised.

Public policy recognizes that radio and television, which enter almost every home in the country, can play a major role in relation to the Irish language; and as we have seen the Broadcasting Authority Act requires RTE to promote the national culture generally and the Irish language in particular. It is recognized, however, that 'the amount of Irish which can be used in the radio and television services is governed also by the other factors involved in national broadcasting including its financial basis, the competition for listeners and viewers, the level of public understanding and acceptance of Irish and the extent to which these services must draw on external sources for programme material'.[29] A major advance, however, has been made with the establishment in March 1972 of an Irish-language broadcasting station, Radio na Gaeltachta. The new service has its own *comhairle* (council) within the general framework of the Broadcasting Authority Act; initially it was available only to the *Gaeltacht* areas but it is now being extended to the community at large on VHF. These developments 'should be seen as creating the opportunity to bring the authentic Gaeltacht day after day to the whole community' and promoting 'one of the main objects of the Government's policy: that the cultural value of the language . . . should become better known to the Irish people'.[30]

REFERENCES

1. Martin D. Carter, *An Introduction to Mass Communications*, p. 22–5, London, Macmillan & Co., 1971.
2. The then Prime Minister, Mr Jack Lynch, T. D., in *Eolas*, Vol. 1, No. 1, April 1972. (Government Information Bureau.)
3. The then Prime Minister, Mr Jack Lynch, T. D., in a speech to the World Congress of the International Federation of Journalists, 29 April 1968.
4. Siegmann, in *Human Rights and Mass Communication*, p. 3, Salzburg, Council of Europe, 1968.
5. Committee on Industrial Progress, op. cit., p. 99.
6. ibid., p. 97.
7. Quoted in *Irish Times*, 24 February 1973.
8. Committee on Industrial Organisation, *Report on the Paper and Paperboard Industry*, p. 8, Dublin, Stationery Office, 1962; Committee on Industrial Progress, op. cit., p. 187.
9. The then Prime Minister, Mr Jack Lynch, T. D., speech to World Congress of the International Federation of Journalists, 29 April 1968.
10. Michael Adams, 'Censorship: The Irish Experience', *Dublin Scepter*, 1971, p. 192.
11. ibid., p. 188.
12. Statement from Irish Pen Club in *Irish Times*, 13 March 1972.
13. National Adult Education Survey, *Interim Report*, p. 143, Dublin, Stationery Office, 1970.
14. Mairin O'Byrne, 'Libraries and Librarianship in Ireland', *Administration*, Vol. 16, No. 2, 1968, p. 152, 155.
15. *Report of the Film Industry Committee*, op. cit., p. 10, 30.
16. ibid., p. 42.
17. 'A view of Irish broadcasting' prepared by the RTE Authority, 1971 and published in the *Irish Times*, 3 January 1973.
18. Quoted in Dowling, Doolan, and Quinn, *Sit Down and be Counted—The Cultural Evolution of a Television Station*, p. 75, Dublin, Wellington Publishers Ltd, 1969.
19. 'A view of Irish broadcasting', op. cit.
20. Quoted in the *Irish Times*, 13 September 1972.
21. David Thornley, 'Television and Politics', *Administration*, Vol. 15, No. 3, 1967, p. 217.
22. The then Prime Minister, Sean Lemass, T.D., *Dail Debates*, Vol. 224, Cols 1045–46, 12 October 1966. (Dublin, Stationery Office.)
23. Gorham, op. cit., p. 328.
24. Jay Blumler, quoted in Chubb, 'Media and the State', *Irish Times*, 31 August 1972.
25. *The Restoration of the Irish Language*, p. 4, Dublin, Stationery Office, 1965.
26. *Report of the Commission on the Restoration of the Irish Language 1958–63*, p. 14, 84, Dublin, Stationery Office, 1963.
27. ibid., p. 86–7.
28. *Report of the Film Industry Committee*, op. cit., p. 36.
29. *The Restoration of the Irish Language*, op. cit., p. 142.
30. *RTE Annual Report, 1970–71*, p. 3; *The Restoration of the Irish Language*, op. cit., p. 142.

4 Policies of the mass media

4.1 The press

The press in Ireland is a free private-enterprise press; State law and fiscal policy obviously impinge upon it, to the extent noted in the previous chapter, but over-all it is not subject to State intervention nor is it generally in receipt of State aid.

The press comprises two largely distinct sectors: the national press—the morning dailies, evenings and the Sunday papers—and the provincial press—for the most part weekly or, occasionally, bi-weekly.

Four newspaper publishing companies make up the national press: Independent Newspapers Ltd, which accounts for the *Irish Independent,* the *Evening Herald* and the *Sunday Independent*; The Irish Press Ltd, which accounts for the *Irish Press, The Evening Press* and the *Sunday Press*; The Irish Times Ltd, which publishes the *Irish Times*; The Cork Examiner Ltd, which accounts for the *Cork Examiner,* and the *Evening Echo.*

The *Cork Examiner* is a family owned, private company; the others are public companies. In the case of the Independent group ownership of the limited number of 'A' shares covers voting control; the preponderance of shares confers only a financial interest. In March 1973 control of the Independent group changed hands through the acquisition of the 'A' shares. In the case of the *Irish Times* the ordinary stock is held entirely by the members of the board and confers an absolute majority of voting shares; the *Irish Times* has announced that it is considering reorganization. In the case of the Irish Press papers the founding family retains a strong interest in a share capital that is otherwise widely diffused, for the most part among small holders, and as trustee and representative of the American company, Irish Press Incorporated, on the board of directors, hold a controlling interest. The Independent and Press groups are, in the context of the Irish market, mass circulation papers selling over the country as a whole. The *Irish Times* on the other hand sells most heavily in the Dublin area which contains according to that paper 'an undue proportion of the country's commercial, professional, academic and cultural elites'.[1] There are, however, no clearly separated 'quality' and 'popular' sectors within the Irish press; a Sunday popular tabloid, the *Sunday Review,* was launched in 1957 but died in 1963. A new Irish Sunday popular paper, the *Sunday World,* appeared in March 1973 published by a company already engaged in publishing magazines and periodicals. The circulation of British newspapers in Ireland, however, does contribute something of a quality/popular dichotomy to the newspaper market. The Cork Examiner papers might be viewed as regional rather than national newspapers as over 95 per cent of their readership is in the southern province of Munster; however they have a national/international, as well as a regional, news focus and are not local papers in the sense in which that term equates with the provincial weekly press.

According to the report of the Committee on Industrial Progress a newspaper though 'only one product . . . has a dual purpose . . . that of providing news and selling advertising space';[2] this is reflected in its two distinct sources of revenue: sales and advertising. 'While the yield from both these markets can vary from newspaper to newspaper generally speaking more than 50 per cent of the revenue comes from advertising.' The committee was of the opinion that in the long term, however, 'circulation and readership are the major factors in determining the volume of advertising . . . and editorial content determines to a great extent the volume of copy sales'. The committee's report noted that 'the content of the paper appears to be exclusively the preserve of the editorial side of management in which the circulation and advertising people have little part to play'.[3] The national newspapers would then appear to enjoy considerable editorial freedom though only the *Irish Times* accords its editor the formal recognition of a place on the board. Following the take-over of Independent Newspapers Ltd, assurances were given that the company and its subsidiaries (see Section 4.7), recognized the rights of editorial freedom and the responsibility of journalists to their professional code of conduct (see Section 5.4). In addition a committee representative of management, editors and journalists is to be established within the company in recognition of 'the special position of journalists in the production of newspapers and the special relationship between a free press and the community'.[4]

A major problem facing the national press is that technological advance may, within the next ten to fifteen years, render much of the present machinery of the newspaper obsolete. Some are now faced with the task of making adequate financial provision to equip themselves for innovation and to meet the challenge of the expanding magazine sector, the introduction of colour television and innovations in the British press which enjoy greater economies of scale. Although the Independent Group has already made progress in this area, particularly with the introduction of colour facilities, the Committee on Industrial Progress was of the opinion that generally the scale of investment required to compete technologically will provide major difficulties for Irish newspapers: this was the basis of its recommendation of adaptation grants and is a partial basis of the newspapers' own demands for taxation relief.

The provincial press shares much of the ethos and character of the national press, in addition to its own particular concerns. It too serves the dual purpose of providing news and selling advertising space; the local newspaper is the traditional medium for the circulation of local news and local advertisements. Due to limited circulation and, in most cases, weekly

3

publication, advertising is a far more extensive source of revenue than copy sales; in addition provincial newspaper publishers engage considerably in job printing which on average accounts for between 30 and 40 per cent of total revenue.

The provincial press fulfils a major social and democratic role outside the urban centres of Dublin and Cork; their penetration of the countryside, particularly of the farming community, is rivalled only by the Sunday newspapers; but of their nature the provincial papers deal far more fully with local news and issues and presumably therefore exercise a greater influence. They play a 'vital part in ensuring that legitimate regional interests are aired and given proper consideration both locally and by central authorities; it is the local paper which makes a town or district articulate, sustaining a sense of local pride and acting as a spur to local development'.[5]

The provincial newspaper sector comprised (in 1970) thirty-seven firms publishing a total of forty-one papers. The Committee on Industrial Progress noted that only a minority are housed in premises specially built for newspaper production and that in the majority of cases the premises are unsuitable for efficient production. On the other hand, some of the more prosperous local newspapers have made considerable technological advances including in some cases the introduction of web-offset printing, colour facilities and computerized type-setting. The committee commented on the danger of over-capacity if technological modernization was not linked with rationalization in the industry as a whole. It reported that 'in some circumstances local markets are possibly over supplied with local newspapers and some rationalization of the newspaper industry might . . . in fact be quite desirable' from an economic viewpoint. In view of the potential social loss involved in newspaper closures it emphasized the aspect of rationalization of production facilities, through associations on a regional basis and the combined use of central printing works. 'This would still leave each paper free to pursue an independent editorial policy . . . in accordance with the tradition of independence which is such a marked feature of provincial newspaper production in Ireland'.[6]

Although editorial freedom is highly valued, political allegiances, where they exist among the provincial press, do so for the most part in muted form. Provincial newspapers are essentially community newspapers; a former President of the Provincial Newspapers Association has written: 'there is a close personal relationship between the people who actually edit and publish provincial newspapers and their readers. Editors and proprietors cannot go out on a limb about local matters without being challenged pretty directly and this undoubtedly engenders a keen sense of responsibility. In turn this must be largely responsible for the confidence that people have in the local paper'.[7] This may now be changing due to the acquisition of several provincial papers by Dublin-based publishers.

4.2 Publishing

One of the major difficulties confronting Irish publishing has been the lack of a consistent publishing tradition; but publishing in Ireland has been expanding since the middle of the 1950s. Between 1967 and 1969 the number of recorded titles published in Ireland (including Northern Ireland) more than doubled from 424 to 992; the number of publishers in the Republic of Ireland grew from approximately 120 to 190. Many of these, however, are primarily printers rather than publishers; in 1968 as many as 108 published a single title only; the number of firms publishing ten titles or more was eleven. The industry has, however, been moving towards larger groupings, including in some cases association with international publishers; this has not only facilitated rationalization of production methods but has encouraged increasing specialization in product policy.

Irish book publishing is heavily orientated towards works by Irish authors in the non-fiction area generally. Irish fiction in English has traditionally been published by the big London houses, and the provision of inexpensive popular paperback literature is almost exclusively an import trade. The market for general interest periodicals too is largely dominated by the internationally established news magazines and attempts to sustain new Irish publications in this field over the past five years have proved financially hazardous. There has, however, been a growth in the number of domestic technical and professional publications; and Irish publishers are beginning to offer a domestic product for the special-interest-market sectors, starting with women and teenagers.

While on a *per capita* basis the sale of books by native authors on the domestic market compares favourably with the situation elsewhere, the limitation in terms of absolute size of the market and the penetration of entire sectors of it by foreign products means that Irish publishers cannot rely solely on the domestic market and must export substantially to survive and expand. Significantly perhaps from this point of view the Committee on Industrial Progress reported that weak marketing was one of the major problems confronting the publishing industry. Since the report, however, the position has improved; the recently formed Irish Book Publishers Association has encouraged increased co-operation among publishers; a major exhibition of Irish printing and publishing went on display in March 1972 to mark International Book Year, and SAMPLA, a sampler of Irish print and publishing, has been launched under the aegis of the association. Members have also, with the assistance of the Export Board, co-operated in joint promotional ventures abroad and a permanent agency to promote Irish books in the United States has been established. Irish publishers now recognize that by building up an international reputation in a specialized field they can exploit the widespread English-speaking market, alone or by sale of rights to international publishing houses; and that, conversely, they can profitably avail of translation rights from continental productions for the home market. Moreover the future promises development of the audio-visual market.

Publishing in the Irish language has shared in the general expansion over recent years, though the growth rate in the number of firms publishing in Irish and the number of Irish titles has not matched that of the industry over-all. Largely because the risks involved are less extensive, publishing in Irish has tended towards a periodical literature and this has influenced the development of literary forms; short stories, essays, anthologies of poetry and magazines are more extensively produced than books. However, the existence of An Club Leabhar (an Irish-language book club) offering selected publications at reduced prices in return for guaranteed sales provides a measure of security for book publishing in Irish as does the demand for textbooks in the study of Irish at all levels of the educational system.

4.3 Cinema and film

Cinema has for long been a major leisure attraction in Ireland; but both aggregate cinema attendance and the ratio of attendances *per capita* have declined seriously since 1957. This decline would seem to be due primarily to a more diversified pattern of leisure/entertainment expenditure made possible by increased affluence, the rapid expansion in the availability of television and the cost of steeply rising overheads which has closed some cinemas. The decline has not everywhere been uniform; it has been most marked in the provincial urban areas, followed by the provincial rural areas and Dublin city suburbs. It has been least drastic in the Dublin city centre cinemas; these are for the most part 'first release' cinemas and the trend here has been towards more and smaller cinemas with a consequently enhanced range of appeal. As we have seen, a feature-film industry has not yet emerged in Ireland; feature films shown in this country are imports, predominantly from the United States, followed by the United Kingdom, and a small minority from other European countries. Likewise the film-distribution system is controlled by the big film-production companies. This influence is strengthened through participation in cinema ownership although the system of cinema circuits is not highly developed outside the major urban centres and each manager is free for the most part to make his own arrangements with the distributors.

The Film Industry Committee 'gave careful consideration to the question of distribution' and the claim that 'an Irish feature film industry would be strangled at birth . . . because . . . [the films] would be unable to secure international distribution'.[8] However, the committee found that the international pattern of film distribution was changing and that television, art-house cinemas and international film festivals offered outlets not previously available. It also commented on the goodwill shown to Irish (short) film-makers by the distributors on the domestic circuit and concluded that a quota system for Irish films would be unnecessary and undesirable. In addition, in view of the fact that the major film companies were spending large sums on the production of films in Ireland—both at Ardmore Studios and on location—it recommended that their distribution revenue should not be taxed to contribute to an Irish film industry.

The dominance of foreign producers and distributors in the Irish market does not seem to pose really serious problems for Irish exhibitors or audiences. While official information is not available it has been estimated that about 230 feature films were examined under the Censorship of Films legislation in 1971; 90 per cent received a certificate and 30 per cent of all films screened in that year carried general (suitable for all age groups) certificates.

A native short-film-making industry has already developed, largely on a sponsorship basis. Among the major sponsors of short films have been RTE, government departments, State-sponsored bodies, commercial firms and religious communities. It is expected that this source of patronage will remain important for the short-film industry; a group of independent Irish film-makers has welcomed the moves to establish a Film Industry Board which it hopes will act as a central and authoritative adviser to all prospective film sponsors in Ireland.

A contributing influence to the development of film-making in Ireland has been the Cork International Film Festival—recently retitled the Cork Film International—which over the past seventeen years has established itself among the European Film Festivals.

4.4 Radio and television

Radio Telefís Éireann broadcasts on a single television channel and two radio channels, one of which broadcasts exclusively in Irish. The two radio programmes are each broadcast from three medium-frequency transmitters and from five VHF transmitters co-sited with the five main television transmitters. The latter are supplemented by some twenty low-power outlying stations to fill in areas of poor television reception; as a result the reach of its services within the State is comprehensive.

Radio Telefís Éireann, as a State-sponsored body, must operate within the framework of the Broadcasting Authority Acts. Under this legislation ultimate responsibility for the broadcasting service, subject to the reserved power of the minister, rests with the RTE authority. The authority in its submission to the Broadcasting Review Committee, 'A View of Irish Broadcasting', has outlined the following view of its own function:

It carries final responsibility for programmes and takes decisions in relation to capital and current expenditure and policy for long term development. Programme and policy initiatives normally come from the professional broadcasting staff to the Authority for consideration but equally well the Authority, out of its public trustee function, initiates consideration of matters which it sees as vital to the discharge of its responsibilities. The Authority too exercises a review function in regard to the general programme output and the manner in which the programmes, in retrospect, are seen to fulfil RTE's statutory obligations.[9]

Under the authority the Director-General has chief executive responsibility for carrying policy into practice.

Under the provisions of the Broadcasting Authority Acts, RTE derives its revenue chiefly from licence fees and advertising and marginally from miscellaneous sources. The Acts do not lay down any ratio to be observed as between income from licence fees and advertising; however, in the interest of 'public service broadcasting' RTE is concerned at the level of its dependence on advertising which in 1971 accounted for 60 per cent of revenue and the extent to which its income is thus made vulnerable to economic factors which affect the level of advertising. RTE regards it as a major matter of policy that commercial interests should not be capable of influencing the nature of the broadcasting services, the revenue from advertising being in its view a by-product of broadcasting.

On radio, advertising takes the form of sponsored programmes and spot advertising; since the expansion of radio broadcasting hours in 1968 the emphasis has shifted heavily from the former to the latter. On television it takes the form of spot advertising alone. Over-all the permitted maximum of advertising time is 10 per cent of broadcasting hours. RTE was among the first media in the country to draw up a code of standards for advertising. While RTE subscribes to the General Code of Advertising Standards (see Section 5.5) accepted by all the major advertising media, the RTE code sets out additional general principles governing the acceptance and presentation of advertising in broadcasting (see Annex 4.1).

RTE has stated that it would wish to achieve a position in which 60 per cent of its revenue came from licence fees and has asked that there be regular biennial reviews of the licence fee. In any event even with the ongoing-phased introduction of colour it expects a relative slowing down in the rate of growth of television advertising revenue because of the fragmentation of audiences, arising from the more extensive availability of British services in the multi-channel areas.

Ultimately these will extend to one-third of the geographical area of the State and will encompass potentially half of the population. A special service unit, RTE Relays, has been formed to participate in the provision of wired television schemes on a commercial basis in competition with private enterprise. However, returns from this are not expected to make good the potential loss of advertising revenue. In any case in view of its obligation to make provision for its own capital development RTE feels that without a guarantee of regular review of the licence fee coherent long-term planning by the authority is not possible.

The three major injunctions in relation to programme matters contained in the broadcasting legislation have been described in the previous chapter and may be recalled briefly here:

The injunction to impartiality and objectivity: The Director-General of RTE has stated that within the limits of this framework the radio and television services generally feel bound to air 'as many champions for as many causes as possible and . . . to maintain a balance between conflicting points of view over time'.[10]

The responsibility to promote the national culture and the Irish language in particular: Before the transfer of responsibility for the broadcasting services to the RTE authority in 1960, programmes and programme material in Irish had been a feature of the radio service; with this transfer, and with the subsequent inception of the television service by the authority, this was adopted as part of its broadcasting policy. 'Programmes of information, entertainment and discussion in Irish are transmitted for listeners and viewers with a sufficiently good knowledge of Irish to be able to understand the language with ease; bilingual programmes, and occasional items or comments in Irish in the course of programmes in English, are intended for those who welcome the opportunity of keeping in touch with their limited knowledge of Irish and, for those who wish to learn Irish or refresh their knowledge of it, there are programmes on radio and television specially designed with these ends in view. From time to time, programme series have been broadcast in English on radio and television with the specific purpose of stimulating public interest in the Irish language and its place in the contemporary situation.' In the view of the authority, however, 'it is important to bear in mind that problems can arise in reconciling the duty to use the broadcasting service to preserve and develop the national culture and the degree of continuing audience acceptance of such programming. Programmes relating to traditional culture, if given a disproportionate place, could run the risk of creating resentment to the object in view. It is important, therefore, that in dealing with matters specifically in the context of the authority's obligation to the national culture, the emphasis should be on programme quality rather than a passive acknowledgement of such interests by merely providing broadcasting time. This would reject both the proposition that excessive minority claims should override majority interests and the proposition that broadcasting has a duty to please most of the people all of the time.'[11]

The authority views the development of Radio na Gaeltachta as an essential element in the discharge of this responsibility.

The obligation to comply with certain written directives from the Minister for Posts and Telegraphs: The single instance of a ministerial directive to refrain from broadcasting certain matter and RTE's response to it have been dealt with in the context of public policy. With regard to allocating broadcasting time to ministers in relation to their public duties, this has frequently been done and it is standard practice to introduce and identify them as ministerial broadcasts.

4.5 Relations between the mass media and the public

Press, radio and television are the media which have most continuous interaction with the public; very little is known however about the relationships between them and the public. What evidence[12] there is indicates four major factors. First in relation to wealth *per capita* the Irish are big consumers of media output. The 1968 National Readership Survey showed that 81 per cent of all adults read an Irish Sunday newspaper (the figure for Sunday readership is estimated at 90 per cent if British papers are included). The RTE Annual Report 1970/71 indicated that 91 per cent of homes have at least one radio and 22 per cent more than one set; on average these were in use twenty-five hours per week and 70 per cent of adults listen to RTE radio sometime each weekday. Television achieved 75 per cent coverage of households (83 per cent of individuals) and on average was in use thirty hours per week in 1971.

Second, consumption of all media output is lower—sometimes appreciably so—in the economically relatively underdeveloped western regions and, except in the case of the provincial press, in the over-65 age group.

Third, morning and evening newspapers and television programmes are availed of more extensively in urban than in rural areas; the Sunday newspapers circulate evenly as between urban and rural areas and the provincial press is the mainstay of the rural areas.

Fourth, regional and social grade variations—and to some extent these overlap—rather than age group, account for most of the differentiation in preference for particular media and for individual newspapers within the press sector.

The consistent importance of developments in Northern Ireland and the Republic, and their significance for each other, as news topics in the Irish media since 1968 highlights an apparent anomaly in the relations between the mass media and the public in Ireland as a whole. While newspapers from Great Britain have an appreciable circulation in the Republic, this is not the case with Northern Ireland daily newspapers despite the fact that the afternoon paper, the *Belfast Telegraph*, has the largest circulation of any daily newspaper in the island. The availability of British radio programmes, and in the multi-channel areas, of British television programmes, both incorporating regional programmes from Northern Ireland does provide a limited amount of Northern-originated material in addition to the comprehensive reporting of the Northern correspondents of the Republic's press and broadcasting services. Conversely sales in Northern Ireland of national newspapers published in the Republic are a tiny fraction of total sales; RTE in its submission to the Broadcasting Review Committee has drawn attention to the unsatisfactory limits of reception of its radio and television programmes in Northern Ireland.

A decision has already been taken to erect a 500kW medium-wave transmitter which is expected to give coverage to the whole country. International agreement is being sought for a frequency for a television transmitter which would provide RTE reception in the more populous north-eastern part of Northern Ireland; reception in the western less-populated part of Northern Ireland is already reasonably adequate.

Very little research has been done in an Irish context on the effectiveness of the mass media. A study[13] of Irish farmers' use of information sources in relation to agricultural innovation showed that the mass media were an important element in creating awareness of new ideas and practices; but farmers tended to rely increasingly on local advisory or informal sources for evaluation and decision. Sixty per cent of farmers named the mass media as a source of first awareness of new techniques generally; but in cases of realized innovations only 27 per cent named the mass media as their initial information source. The authors concluded that this would seem to imply a high degree of mass media wastage. The press rated higher than the broadcasting services as a source of awareness (despite the recognized excellence of RTE's agricultural programmes); but there is no way of knowing whether farmers are representative of the community as a whole in this regard. Within the press sector a specialist publication, *The Farmers Journal*, was named by 28 per cent of farmers as a first-awareness source and was particularly effective with younger, better-educated farmers with better holdings; in terms of realized innovations, however, the general press enjoyed the greater staying power.

Generally the mass media would seem to command a high degree of acceptance among the public. A news inquiry survey undertaken by RTE showed that 72 per cent agreed that one could depend on the news from RTE, as against 13 per cent who disagreed; and although RTE was regarded as a more reliable news source than the newspapers by 77 per cent of respondents (as against 15 per cent who disagreed) the over-all level of trust and appreciation would appear to be high. Results from pilot survey material from the Economic and Social Research Institute's major survey of civic attitudes reveal that while 59 per cent believe that 'ordinary people' have from a little to a great influence on what happens in the Dail, 83 per cent credit 'popular opinion as expressed in the newspapers' with this influence; and only 3 per cent hold that the 'news media' have too much influence over the way government is run. Finally a manpower survey conducted for the Department of Labour in Drogheda, a prosperous east-coast town, has shown that occupations in the mass media—whether secretarial, technical or professional—rated middle to high on a list of valued occupations; more so among young people than among their parents, with post-primary school-leaving girls particularly showing a strong liking for journalism. None of these findings is so comprehensively based as to be definitive but taken together they provide at least an indication of the position as it is known to date.[14]

4.6 Relations between the mass media and sources of information

Official information. First, a great deal of official information reaches the media and the public through the official information agencies whose structures and functions were outlined in chapter 3. Between 1968 and 1972 the average number of queries processed weekly by the Government Information Bureau increased from 250 to 1,000; the number of official documents released increased from 2,500 to 4,000; and the number of departmental information officers doubled from four to eight among the sixteen departments of State. A decision has recently been taken by the government accepting the need for an organizational policy on communications within the structure of the departments of State; a working party has been established to identify the measures necessary for the implementation of such a policy.

Second, more overt 'political' news comes primarily from reports of Oireachtas and local authority debates and of Dail question-time. A key institution in this process is the Oireachtas Press Gallery—an exclusive association of journalists, representing most of the domestic and overseas news organizations who report Oireachtas proceedings and who have informal access to important political figures. In addition each of the four daily newspapers and RTE employs a political correspondent who, while a member of the Press Gallery, has a more interpretive and comment oriented function.

General domestic coverage: In their treatment of official information, as well as in their domestic news coverage generally, the characteristic approach of the Irish media has been responsive and reportive rather than creative. The advent of current affairs television programmes has however fostered a more investigative type of journalism and a report on the RTE newsroom stated recently 'that News as we understand it is facing a crisis of identity . . . traditional news values are being questioned' and criticized the position in which there was 'no attempt at News initiation'.[15] An aspect of this changing emphasis has been the growing use of public opinion polls by Irish newspapers and periodicals as a base for major stories.

International news: The Irish media carry a considerable amount of international news. Much of this is British news and RTE and the national newspaper groups maintain their own bureaux in London; in addition there are now Irish correspondents based in Brussels and there is also a growing use of syndicated material from that source. A great deal of foreign news is, however, derived from the news agencies which may be explained and interpreted by resident correspondents, either the foreign correspondent or the relevant functional specialist. The main agencies serving the Irish media are British and American: on the one hand Press Association-Reuters and Exchange Telegraph Co., and on the other the Associated Press and United Press International. In addition the *Irish Times* makes extensive use of Times News & Feature Services. Some of the international agencies retain either a staff reporter or a correspondent in Dublin. There is no Irish news agency. However, RTE as a member of the European Broadcasting Union contributes to and is a customer of the Eurovision network and the Eurovision News Exchange Service; it also draws on the international news and newsfilm agencies and is a party to the Washington agreements governing participation in international satellite transmissions. RTE has been a major source of information on the Irish situation over the past four years, its material being taken and retransmitted regularly by broadcasting organizations throughout Europe and elsewhere.

4.7 Relations between the various media

There is a clear distinction between the broadcasting services which are publicly owned and the press which is privately owned. The press itself is not heavily 'concentrated'; the national newspaper groups, though they are associated for certain industrial relations purposes and while the Dublin-based ones co-operate in distribution arrangements to the more remote regions, are structurally independent and compete for circulation and advertising. Domestic periodical production is in turn largely independent of the newspaper structure, here too, apart from one extensive group which recently commenced publication of a Sunday newspaper (see Section 4.1), chain systems have not widely developed.

The provincial press has traditionally been family owned but some changes have been occurring in this sector in recent years. The major change has been the acquisition by Independent Newspapers of two provincial newspaper groups and two other newspapers. Other groupings exist on a small scale. In view of the small circulation of many provincial newspapers some process of rationalization or attrition in this sector was probably inevitable; but some of the papers involved in recent dealings have been among the more substantial in the provincial sector. A new development in urban centres has been the advent of local weekly papers entirely supported by advertising.

As information and entertainment media, press and broadcasting would seem to be used complementarily by the public. Television has, however, challenged the press in a number of ways.

For example, although between 1961 and 1968 advertising revenue expended on the press increased, as a percentage of total advertising expenditure it fell from 82 per cent to 51 per cent while that spent on television rose from 2 per cent to 32 per cent. While the position has not appreciably changed in recent years the Committee on Industrial Progress indicated that it expects that colour television from Irish television—already a reality in respect of film and outside broadcasts but not in respect of studio-originated programmes or advertising—and the more widespread availability of British commercial television will pose fresh problems for the press.

In addition the press has met the challenge of television news—striking in its immediacy but lacking deep penetration— by appointing specialists in many fields and insisting on coverage in depth; while television has not rendered the newspaper obsolete as a vehicle of hard news it has clearly promoted the development of analysis and comment in the press.

Finally television journalism has attracted established journalists from the press sector and is now a major competitor in the recruitment of new entrants to the media.

Competition from the British mass media—which operate on a far greater scale with far greater resources—is also a serious problem for the Irish mass media. Between 1963 and 1969 the British newspapers' share of the Irish daily and Sunday market rose from 12 per cent to 18 per cent; and since 1963 the British television services have raised their combined share of the multi-channel audience from 33 per cent to approximately 45 per cent; as a percentage of total domestic audience the multi-channel audience is still growing.

Annex 4.1 **RTE Code of standards for advertising**

The basic principle governing the acceptance and presentation of television advertising by the authority is that it should be legal, honest, truthful and within the accepted bounds of good taste. By general agreement this criterion already applies to all reputable advertising within the State, in media other than television. But it will be obvious that the unique position of television, as a medium which penetrates intimately into the home and family circle, raises special problems in this field and demands the maintenance of unusually high standards in relation to the acceptance and presentation of advertising material.

Because of the unique power of television as a medium of communication, the authority and all advertisers making use of the medium must accept a high degree of responsibility towards the family and the community in general—particularly with regard to the special needs of children, community responsibility for the advancement of education and culture, decency and decorum in the production and propriety in the presentation of advertising.

REFERENCES

1. *Commentary on the national readership survey in Ireland (1968)*, p. 5, presented by The Irish Times Ltd, 1969.
2. Committee on Industrial Progress, op. cit., p. 100.
3. ibid, p. 101, 106.
4. Reported in *Irish Independent,* 19 March 1973.
5. Dr J. F. Dempsey, 'The Role of the Press', quoted in Nolan, op. cit., p. 15.
6. Committee on Industrial Progress, op. cit., p. 97, 98, 120.
7. Nolan, op. cit., p. 25.
8. *Report of the Film Industry Committee,* op. cit., p. 14.
9. 'A view of Irish broadcasting', op. cit.
10. T. P. Hardiman, Director-General of RTE, quoted in Dowling, *et al.,* op. cit., Appendix III, p. xliv.
11. 'A view of Irish broadcasting', op. cit.
12. Sources: National readership survey, 1968; *RTE Annual Report 1970/71;* A view of Irish broadcasting'.
13. Bohlen and Breathnach, 'Irish Farmers' Use of Information Sources', *Irish Journal of Agricultural Economics and Rural Sociology,* Vol. 3, No. 1, 1970.

14. Sources: RTE news inquiry quoted in Chubb, op. cit., p. 140; pilot material from general survey of attitudes and values in Ireland (Economic and Social Research Institute, Dublin, unpublished); Conor Ward, *Manpower in a Developing Community—Drogheda,* Dublin, Department of Labour, 1966.
15. Burns and Liston, 'Survey of RTE News Division', p. 2, 8 (unpublished).
16. 'A view of Irish broadcasting', op. cit.

5 Communication professions

5.1 Introduction

The communications industry comprises a large number of specialized agencies, all interdependent. Communicators are people with a wide range of backgrounds and skills working in the press, publishing, film and cinema, radio and television—the major functional areas dealt with in this monograph. Beyond these there are the ancillary activities such as printing, block-making, photography, designing and others, and the commercial services of marketing, market research, advertising and public relations which in relation to the mass media might be regarded as secondary activities which at once provide supports and constitute demands. Apart then from a brief reference to the growth of advertising and public relations it has seemed best to concentrate on the career of journalist rather than undertake an anecdotal survey of all aspects of this multifaceted industry. This career is more highly developed than most other 'communication professions' and involves also the greatest degree of direct and recurring contact with the public.

5.2 Professional training

In Ireland there was until recently no established pattern of recruitment to journalism. Traditionally entry has been at school-leavers age followed by on-the-job training; service with the provincial press before moving to a daily paper would be usual. There have of course been openings for graduates who possess specialist skills and qualifications which would enable them to enter into a particular aspect of journalism. The demand for graduates has increased with growing specialization in reporting as newspapers and the broadcasting services increasingly provide detailed interpretative background to the regular news bulletins and as the specialist sectors of the media extend beyond economics and finance to include science, medicine, religion and foreign affairs, among others. Journalists have none the less a long-established identity as a professional group. Members of the National Union of Journalists—the major trade union catering for Irish journalists—subscribe to a code of professional conduct (Annex 5.1) and the Census of Population lists journalism among the professional occupations. Developments in broadcast journalism with the introduction of television and a revolution in the coverage of

46

news generally over the past decade have, however, focused attention in Ireland as elsewhere on the extent to which journalism can be called a profession; and in general it has been a time of growing professional consciousness in Irish journalism. Journalism recruitment and training is increasingly being formalized and a domestic investigation of the RTE newsroom criticized 'the mystique news staff attach to the news selection process . . . and the emphasis on having a news nose'; the memorandum emphasized the priority of training 'on an ongoing—refresher—retraining basis'.[1]

For non-graduates a professional course in journalism is now provided at the School of Journalism, College of Commerce, Dublin, for school-leavers proposing to enter journalism. The course initiated by the Irish branch of the British-based National Council for the Training of Journalists, a body representing employer, managerial, trade union and educational interests, is directed by a former editor of the *Irish Independent*. The school, while insisting that journalism can be learned only through experience, aims to provide 'a general education of third-level standard in subjects of special value to journalists'.[2] The director, however, has pointed out some of the disadvantages still attaching to the scheme—a single academic year has been found to be too short and as from 1973 the course will be of two years' duration; ultimately he would like to see the course recognized as qualifying for a diploma of equivalent status to a university degree. Completion of the course does not guarantee employment in journalism, while attempts to make it mandatory for non-graduates entering journalism have met with substantial but not full success.

The term 'professional' might be thought to include two main attributes: '. . . one is being skilled in one's job—skill which comes from training and sustained experience. The other is having the fundamental knowledge of and deep familiarity with a subject which enables a man to move with ease among its concepts'.[3] It is the absence of any systematic body of theory and a well-defined professional culture that is the major obstacle to complete professionalization. This is not to deny that journalists have a clear conception of professional responsibility, it is rather to state that 'professionals are allowed a considerable amount of freedom from direct control in return for internal regulation of members' conduct by the professional group itself' and 'there appears to be a widespread opinion that the rules of operation governing the behaviour of communicators should be *visible*'[4] in the sense of being explicit defined and elaborated: particularly when the group has a high potential ability to influence other people. The absence of any detailed appreciation of the communicators' code, tested against behaviour, might arguably have serious consequences for the relationship of trust between communicators and public.

One way in which the conception of 'professional responsibility' might be elaborated is through the accumulation of case studies of journalistic conduct. An example is the study *Demonstrations and Communication: A Case Study*, which examined the treatment in the media of a protest march, carried out by the Centre for Mass Communication Research, University of Leicester (United Kingdom). A study along similar lines—an analysis of the content of both British and Irish media reporting of the Northern Ireland situation, based on a fortnight in November 1971—is currently being undertaken by the centre. The need for regular studies of this kind might be viewed as part of the general need for systematic communication studies referred to in Chapter 6. Alternatively the proposition that there ought to be at least one Chair of Journalism in our universities has occasionally been advocated within the profession and by at least one prominent political figure.

5.3 Journalistic behaviour

Within a generally favourable environment, as indicated for instance in Section 4.5, the question of proper journalistic conduct has come in for discussion a number of times in the past five years.

The Report of the Committee on the Constitution (1967) concerned itself with all aspects of parliamentary privilege including the particular question of 'improper press comment'. It noted that 'the Dail in the past has treated this as an interference but in over forty years it has dealt formally with only three cases, two of which involved statements by members themselves. In the third case . . . the Committee on Procedures and Privileges decided that the dignity of the House was best served by ignoring the matter'.[5] This procedure was again adopted in a more recent case. The Report made available a good deal of comparative material on this issue.

The Judical Tribunal established by the Taoiseach in November 1969 to inquire into a television programme (cf. Section 3.6) was asked to consider, *inter alia,* the planning, preparation, arrangement, production and presentation of the programme; the authenticity of the programme; the adequacy of the information on which the programme was based, and whether the statements, comments and implications of the programme reflected reasonable journalistic care on the part of those responsible for the programme. The tribunal took evidence from three senior Irish journalists on the question of journalistic standards. From the evidence of these three witnesses it derived principles relevant to the standard of journalistic care in the presentation of facts (cf. Annex 5.2); '. . . we consider that there was a (partial) failure to apply these principles'.[6] The tribunal adverted to the question of the invasion of privacy, but refrained from any judgement on the matter on the grounds that the subject was arguably outside the terms of reference of the tribunal, and that the matter might ultimately be the subject of international convention and have to be dealt with by legislation.

The Ministerial directive to RTE under Section 31 of the Broadcasting Act in October 1971 brought strong protests then and since from journalists who claimed that their 'duty to the Irish people was to present news and interpret its current significance'.[7]

In November 1972 an RTE journalist was sentenced to three months in jail for contempt of court for refusing to identify in an absolutely positive manner the interviewee in a tape recording the substance of which he had broadcast, when the tape was before the court as evidence. The journalist claimed privilege in the protection of sources. The sentence is being appealed. The previous case of a journalist being jailed for contempt occurred in 1933. The case was followed by a series of short protest strikes by some journalists. Simultaneously some journalists protested against the provisions of the newly published Offences Against the State (Amendment) Bill which appeared to them potentially restrictive.

An interesting if isolated episode—which strictly was not an issue of journalistic conduct—occurred in May 1972 when an issue of the fortnightly *Hibernia National Review* appeared without its customary back page satire. Members of the Irish Graphical Society had refused to print 'text and illustrations [that] were a satire on the Church and offensive to good taste'.[8] The issue was seen largely as one of censorship but the general secretary of the society argued that the issue of individual responsibility for upholding standards was also involved. The editor had offered to carry a disclaimer on behalf of the society but this was not acceptable.

Two more general concerns also arise in respect of journalistic behaviour. The first has been raised persistently by journalists themselves: it relates to the necessity to uphold professional standards against the commercial demands of the time, to help create a more critical and informed public and to avoid making too many concessions to popular taste. The other relates to the issue of a potential tension between the industrial rights of management and unions in the mass media and the public interest in open communications. In the case of the three Dublin daily newspaper publishers, for example, there exists an arrangement which is the subject of criticism whereby if any of them is closed by an industrial dispute all three cease to publish. The operation of the agreement has for some time been under discussion between the companies. On the other hand criticism has been levelled at the insistence of journalists that, as a general principle, practice in the media should be exclusively reserved to professionals. Debate on the issue seems likely to intensify: the Director-General of RTE recently questioned 'Whether the traditional concept of professional control . . . was becoming outmoded and even inimical to proper community communications'[9], at least in the case of radio and television which are publicly owned and, technologically, offer the best prospects of broader participation.

5.4 Codes of ethics and traditions

Three professional groups cater for Irish journalists. The vast majority of these are members of the Irish section of the British-based National Union of Journalists (NUJ); it draws its members from press, broadcasting and certain branches of publicity and public relations and thus helps create a common professional ethos across a range of media. Numbers 10–15 inclusive of its sixteen-point Code of Professional Conduct (Annex 5.1) might be regarded as overtly ethical, as distinct from professional, in concern. In addition there

4

are fairly widely held assumptions among practitioners as to the qualities that properly pertain to a good journalist; among them are 'mental and physical agility . . . moral and physical courage . . . discrimination, sound judgement, a balanced mind . . . ability, integrity and experience . . . honesty, fairness, balance and accuracy'.[10]

Within this shared consensus, however, there exists the possibility of great variation of emphasis. This variation may explain the belief that journalists have traditionally been easier to organize around issues of pay and work conditions than around issues of professional control. In particular three programme producers who resigned from RTE in 1969 claimed that 'union intervention [in this case, Irish Actors Equity Association] on a matter of ethics and morals was obviously difficult. Their traditional role—to seek better wages and conditions—while not making it impossible for them to be involved in matters of professional conduct nevertheless raised problems in the specialized and complicated field of television communications'.[11] As against that, the NUJ has strongly defended its members' professional interests in various controversies referred to in this chapter.

In these circumstances it is perhaps not surprising that the idea of a press council—a source of non-binding normative regulation—canvassed now for a number of years should receive new prominence. The idea of a press council has growing, but by no means universal, support among journalists. The original suspicion of a council as a control instrument has moderated as the proposal is endorsed by recognized civil liberties advocates and representatives of journalists themselves. The Chairman of Amnesty International and a former Secretary General of the International Commission of Jurists, advised journalists: 'The Press Council in England has worked well and has proved useful both to the public and the press . . . rather than tolerate governmental interference . . . a measure of self-discipline under the supervision of an Irish Press Council would help secure the independence of the press and media more fully . . . the initiative should come from journalists themselves'.[12]

The NUJ now 'readily accepts that a Press Council should consider complaints against individual journalists or media alleging inaccurate, unfair or unbalanced reporting or comment. But if there is to be a Press Council it will have to be a proper one having constructive and protective rules. Its functions should include that of being a watchdog on proposed newspaper mergers and takeovers'.[13] The problem of 'concentration' is not at present a major feature of the press in Ireland; as we have seen, the CIP report (1970) suggested that some degree of rationalization in the provincial newspaper industry might be useful.

The Irish Transport and General Workers Union has argued that radio and television should come within the ambit of a press council. There have also been suggestions of a separate broadcasting council. A novel variation on this theme is the suggestion that 'news and current affairs broadcasting be separated from the rest of broadcasting. It should be placed under the control of an independent board . . .—anchored within the ambit of the journalistic profession and presided over by members of that profession—. . .

that knows when to stand firm on professional grounds and to insist on professional standards in the work of its staff'.[14] This proposal, which would constitute a major departure from the provisions of the current broadcasting legislation, has not so far elicited any public response, favourable or otherwise.

5.5 Advertising and public relations

Among the major growth areas in the communication professions in Ireland are advertising and public relations.

In the decade 1958–68 the amount of spending on advertising in Ireland quadrupled—the volume of advertising almost doubled—until it amounted to 1 per cent of GNP. The greatest part of this increase was expended on the new television service; since 1968 spending on this medium has levelled off and the increased spending has been directed to periodicals and below-the-line advertising. The Association of Advertisers in Ireland Ltd is the protective, consultative and advisory organization entitled to speak on behalf of advertisers in Ireland; its aims are to protect the interests of advertisers and to promote sound ethical and economic principles in the industry. It is responsible for the Code of Advertising Standards first produced in 1967 and now in its third revised edition. The purpose of the code is 'to formalize existing practices relative to advertising in Ireland and to define practices considered undesirable'; it requires that 'all advertising in all media should be legal, decent, honest and truthful'.[15] The code is administered by an Advertising Standards Committee with representatives from advertising and the mass media and an independent chairman.

Although the State-sponsored Electricity Supply Board is believed to have been the first public enterprise in Europe to appoint, in 1928, a public relations officer, it is only with the development of industry and commerce in the past fifteen years that a public relations sector has become firmly established. Most of the major advertising agencies have now got their own public relations department. The Public Relations Institute of Ireland, founded in 1953, is the co-ordinating body for those professionally engaged in public relations—'the planned and sustained effort to establish and maintain mutual understanding between an organization and its public';[16] currently it has over 250 members. The objects of the institute are to prescribe and foster high professional standards, to give a united voice to the practitioners of public relations in Ireland, to promote general appreciation of the principles and practices of their profession and to sponsor specialized training courses.

Annex 5.1 Code of Professional Conduct of the National Union of Journalists

1. A member should do nothing that would bring discredit on himself, his union, his newspaper, or his profession. He should study the rules of his

51

union, and should not by commission or omission, act against the interests of the union.

2. Unless the employer consents to a variation, a member who wishes to terminate his employment must give notice, according to agreement or professional custom.

3. No member should seek promotion or seek to obtain the position of another journalist by unfair methods.

4. A member should not, directly or indirectly, attempt to obtain for himself, or anyone else any commission, regular or occasional, held by a freelance member of the union. A member should not accept a commission normally held by a freelance member of the union without reasonable cause.

5. It is unprofessional conduct to exploit the labour of another journalist by plagiarism, or by using his copy for linage purposes without permission.

6. Staff men who do linage work should be prepared to give up such work to conform with any pooling scheme approved by the National Executive Council, or any union plan to provide a freelance member with a means of earning a living.

7. A member holding a staff appointment shall serve first the paper that employs him. In his own time a member is free to engage in other creative work, but he should not undertake any extra work in his rest time or holidays if by so doing he is depriving an out-of-work member of a chance to obtain employment.

8. While a spirit of willingness to help other members should be encouraged at all times, members are under a special obligation of honour to help an unemployed member to obtain work.

9. Every journalist should treat subordinates as considerately as he would desire to be treated by his superiors.

10. Freedom in the honest collection and publication of news facts and the rights of fair comment and criticism, are principles which every journalist should defend.

11. A journalist should fully realize his personal responsibility for everything he sends to his paper or agency. He should keep union and professional secrets, and respect all necessary confidences regarding sources of information and private documents. He should not falsify information or documents, or distort or misrepresent facts.

12. In obtaining news or pictures, reporters and press photographers should do nothing that will cause pain or humiliation to innocent, bereaved, or otherwise distressed persons. News, pictures, and documents should be acquired by honest methods only.

13. Every journalist should keep in mind the dangers in the laws of libel, contempt of court and copyright. In reports of law court proceedings it is necessary to observe and practise the rule of fair play to all parties.

14. Whether for publication or suppression the acceptance of a bribe by a journalist is one of the gravest professional offences.

15. A journalist shall not, in the performance of his professional duties, lend himself to the distortion or suppression of the truth because of advertising considerations.

16. Except in the case of freelances, reporters should not take photographs and photographers should not report other than in exceptional circumstances.

Annex 5.2 **Report of Tribunal of Enquiry into the Television Programme on Illegal Moneylending**

'Principles relevant to the standard of journalistic care in the presentation of facts':

1. A journalist must make every effort to ensure that the facts he presents are true and accurate.
2. To do this he should try to check the facts at every possible stage.
3. Where it is not possible to check the facts, he should evaluate critically the source from which they come.
4. While he may accept statements from obviously reliable and trustworthy sources, he should be doubtful about information of a factual nature which he cannot check coming from a source which is not shown by experience or otherwise to be reliable and accurate.
5. The evaluation of such a source involves checking into the background of the informant, his means of knowledge and his reputation for veracity.
6. Where an editor, or other journalist responsible for the presentation of fact, relies on the investigation and judgement of a subordinate or researcher, he must be satisfied as to the experience of that person and his suitability for the task.

REFERENCES

1. Burns and Liston, op. cit., p. 2, 13.
2. Louis McRedmond, *The School of Journalism,* College of Commerce (unpub–lished).
3. HMSO, *The Civil Service (The Fulton Report),* Vol. 1, p. 16, London, HMSO, 1968.
4. *Modern Communications and Community Development,* p. 25, Tipperary, Muintir na Tire', 1966; Oliver Boyd-Barret, 'Journalism Recruitment and Training—Problems in Professionalization', in Jeremy Tunstall (ed), *Media Sociology,* p. 185, London, Constable, 1970.
5. *Report of the Committee on the Constitution,* op. cit., p. 15.
6. *Report of the Moneylending Tribunal,* p. 79.
7. Quoted in *Irish Independent,* 17 June 1972.
8. Quoted in *Irish Times,* 26 May 1972.
9. T. P. Hardiman, quoted in *Irish Times,* 21 November 1972.
10. Respectively:
Michael McDonagh, 'The Influence of Press, Radio and Television', *Christus Rex* (Dublin), Vol. 16, No. 2, 1962, p. 112; McRedmond, op. cit.; Miles O'Farrell, 'Transcript of Evidence to Moneylending Tribunal', para. 4967, Dublin, National Library; T. P. Coogan, ibid, para. 5001.

11. Dowling *et al.*, op. cit., p. 99.
12. Sean McBride, quoted in *Irish Times*, 4 December 1971.
13. Patrick Nolan (NUJ) quoted in *Irish Independent*, 8 July 1972.
14. Chubb, 'Media and State', *Irish Times*, 31 August 1972.
15. 'Code of Advertising Standards for Ireland', p. 2.
16. Brochure of the Public Relations Institute of Ireland.

6 Social participation

6.1 Introduction

A major problem of modern communications relates to how individuals, social groups and voluntary organizations can make their voices heard in shaping the functioning of the mass communication system. Fundamentally, the awareness of this possibility derives from 'a growing appreciation of two central facts about mass communication: firstly, mass communications operate in conjunction with existing channels and patterns of communication which are themselves already determined by the positioning of individuals and groups in a social structure; secondly, the actions of communicator and recipient in a mass communication system are determined by their place in the social system as a whole . . . both are subject to constraints and the actions of both are always liable to patterning and control'.[1] The problem is particularly associated with press, radio and television which tend to be regarded as the crucial media. Opportunities for influence might be best considered in three different contexts.

6.2 Opportunities for influence: public policy

In the first place there are the opportunities which arise in the execution of public policy. These include: the raising of matters of citizen concern by public representatives by way of parliamentary and local authority debate and parliamentary question. Among the matters which have arisen in this way recently are the ethics of advertising, particularly in relation to cigarettes and alcohol; violence in the media; access of juveniles to pornographic material. In addition the Report of the Oireachtas Committee on the Constitution (1967) and the Judicial Tribunal into the television programme on illegal moneylending (1969) provided the occasion of widespread public debate.

The appointment of representatives of recognizable interests to such bodies as the Television Commission (1958–59), the Film Industry Committee (1967–68) and the Broadcasting Review Committee set up in 1971; and the provision for interested groups or members of the public to give evidence to these bodies. A more limited application of this procedure may be seen in the work of the Committee on Industrial Organization and its successor the Committee on Industrial Progress in relation to the paper and printing industries generally (1962–64; 1970–71). These were limited in that membership was confined to representatives of government, industry and trade unions and their concern was primarily with the economics of these industries. There has been no comprehensive inquiry into the press in Ireland along the lines of the British Royal Commission on the Press between 1947 and 1949.

Recurring opportunities within this *modus operandi* arise with the appointment, from time to time, of members to such as the censorship boards and censorship appeal boards, and to the RTE authority. It is not possible to state definitely whether members are appointed qua individuals or qua representatives of interests; but a government publication on the Irish language in 1966 noted that 'the members of the Radio (Telefís) Éireann Authority appointed in June 1965 included two members of the Irish language consultative council'.[2]

Public policy has particular application in respect of RTE. Section 21 of the Broadcasting Authority Act 1960 provides that 'for the purpose of enabling the Authority to have advice in performing its functions, the Minister, after consultation with the Authority, may from time to time appoint advisory committees or advisers . . . the Authority and the Director-General shall have regard to but shall not be bound by any advice tendered in this way'. The National Youth Council has asked that this provision be used more extensively to allow a fuller participation by the community in the advisory committees of the authority.

Over and above the suggestion of the establishment of specialist advisory committees within the Broadcasting Authority Act there have been suggestions that broadcast matter might come within the ambit of a Press Council, should one be established, or that, alternatively, there might be a Broadcasting Council along similar lines. In either case laymen, as well as professional communicators, would, presumably, sit on the council. The RTE authority has stated that it would welcome an advisory council which 'would provide an informed and representative opinion on the programme output and would also allow for greater public participation in the broadcasting service'.[3]

More generally, the Devlin report remarked on 'the extent to which, in other countries, the public are involved with officials in enquiries that lead to the formulation of new proposals for policy . . . there are many. . . issues where consultation . . . might improve the quality of subsequent decisions and legislation. We recommend that this should be secured by setting up *ad hoc* groups with private and public sector representation to examine all major proposals for policy development. Participation should be seen to operate and if this system does not work, we recommend that councils . . . be set up for . . . five main areas of Government'.[4] Either of these two structures might facilitate public involvement in the formulation of communication policy.

6.3   Opportunities for influence: the media

Secondly, there are opportunities for influence and participation provided by the media themselves. These include access to media coverage as determined by criteria of 'news value', i.e. news selection and presentation. The problem is that while few would disagree that news is selected on the basis of interest and importance there are differing views on what is interesting and what is important and what the ideal mix should be. An attempt to establish some evidence on news policies and practices is currently in progress and RTE has agreed that its news service and the process of news gathering, news selection and dissemination should be studied by social scientists under the auspices of the International Broadcasting Institute in company with the broadcasting services of Sweden and Nigeria. And mention has been made in Chapter 5 of the investigation, involving a study of the Irish media, of reporting on Northern Ireland in November 1971.

Built-in opportunities for response are also provided by the media. Typically these take the form of the letter to the editor, phone-in programmes on radio, right of reply on television and the attempt to recreate the local group as when farmers were brought together at viewing centres to watch agricultural advisory programmes on television. This last, according to the programme presenter, was a deliberate attempt 'to get over the fury that I suppose every television viewer experiences at one time or another when he cannot answer back'.[5] Despite these efforts however a sense of dissatisfaction remains; one professional communicator called attention 'to the sense of frustration, aggravation and annoyance that many people feel towards the mass media. They want to talk back . . . but the present methods of developing dialogue . . . are felt to be inadequate'.[6] It is argued in the case of newspapers that the more local its readership the greater the feedback obtained by the editor; and that a system of local radio might elicit the same response. In this connexion it may be of interest to note that Radio na Gaeltachta has initiated a feedback system. Other suggestions include a greater development of local public relations, the formation of look/listen groups, but a major demand continues to be that some formal machinery for consultation between the programme controllers and the public, or the special-interest groups within it, be established. In the case of RTE the provision for advisory councils within the Broadcasting Act offers a ready-made opportunity.

Audience research by the media also provides for a measure of feedback. RTE uses two means of assessing the preferences of its audiences: Television Audience Measurement Ltd (TAM) ratings and Television Audience Research Service. This is an independent market research organization set up in Britain after the establishment of Independent Television (1954); since 1962 it has been contracted to provide programme ratings for RTE. TAM ratings are an estimate of the percentages of all homes with television which are switched on to a particular station at any given time. The functions of TAM ratings are 'to assess the reach and relative popularity of different

programmes, to demonstrate the message-giving power of the medium to potential advertisers and to assist in determining the rates at which it is fair and
reasonable to charge advertisers' at particular times of the season, week
and day. The TAM service is paid for by RTE, the advertising agencies
and the major advertisers. The TAM service is strictly quantitative, however,
and needs to be complemented by research which investigates opinions and
attitudes towards programmes, particularly those aimed at minority audiences.
This task is undertaken by the Audience Research Department of RTE. A
voluntary panel of listeners and viewers is recruited every four months
and questionnaires, for the most part precoded, are despatched to panel
members every week. Questions relate to a selected list of eighteen radio
and television programmes, 'selected because of their importance, their
novelty and the extent to which they are thought or known to depart from
an acceptable degree of approval by listeners and viewers'.[7] In this way
a more qualitative form of feedback is made available to the programme
controllers.

Circulation figures for virtually all the newspapers—national and
provincial—and for some, but by no means all, of the periodicals and
journals are compiled and published every six months by Audit Bureau of
Circulations Limited (London) (ABC). In addition figures are made available
to the business magazine *Management* on the basis of an auditors' certificate
or publishers' statement. Two national readership surveys have been carried
out in 1956-57 and 1968-69 for the daily newspaper publishers as well as
a readership survey for the Provincial Newspapers Association in 1959-60.
The CIP report (1970) 'would have thought that a national readership
survey would be carried out with much greater frequency', and in fact a
joint readership/viewer survey is at present being undertaken for the national
newspapers and RTE. CIP was of the opinion though that 'these surveys, in
addition to helping papers obtain advertisers, should also be useful in
helping publishers to determine editorial content. None of the newpaper firms
has any formal information on such matters as the image of their papers in
the market, nor have they reader reaction to specific features or even on page
traffic readership counts. All these aspects are amenable to available market
research techniques'.[8] Despite this criticism it remains true that in terms
of quantitative measurement in respect of radio, television and the national
press, the position in Ireland has improved in recent years. There is now,
however, an increasing range of 'intensely individualist periodicals . . . catering
to specialist intellectual or social groups: most of them are unable to afford
the research required to give adequate media evaluation data'.[9] Perhaps
there is a case to be made here for a co-operative venture in research.

Finally, reference has already been made to the possibilities open for lay
participation in a Press Council. Whatever attitude the State adopts to the
idea of a Broadcasting Council for the State-sponsored radio and television
service, the desirability of establishing a Press Council remains largely a
question for media owners and professional communicators in response to
public opinion.

6.4 Opportunities for influence: social groups and institutions

Thirdly, and finally, there are the opportunities for influence and participation which are created by social groups and institutions themselves.

One of the most notable features here is increasing emphasis by all major bodies and institutions on better two-way communications with the public. An outstanding example of this trend might be cited in the case of a body enjoying extensive allegiance among the community. The population of the Republic is overwhelmingly Catholic. The Roman Catholic Hierarchy in response to a directive in the Decree on Social Communications of the Second Vatican Council established, in 1969, the Catholic Communications Institute of Ireland 'to advise the Hierarchy on *communications policy* and to assist the work of communications in the Church by means of research, education and publication in the media'.[10] The institute is governed by a council whose members are chosen for their competence in various fields related to communications; it has its own radio department and film unit, provides training-courses in the use of press, radio and television and markets its own publications through its commercial arm, Veritas Limited.

A continuing debate on the role of the media generally and more particularly of the most recent medium—television—is another example of this process. In its most developed form this debate issues in major seminars, such as those on 'The Challenge of Television', 'The Media of Social Communication', 'Modern Communications and Community Education'; and the annual Communications Conference sponsored by the Public Relations Institute of Ireland. A review of the literature of these gatherings would seem to indicate three particular topics of concern.

First, the need for public participation in the functioning of the mass communication system. In fact these seminars have proved to be among the most fruitful sources of contact between professional communicators, who have supported them admirably, and members of the public.

Second, the nature of the impact and effects of the mass media and the dangers of an uncritical audience. The indications are that many of the present concerns about the effect of the mass media are of long standing and that there is a lack of adequate indigenous communications research. The Director-General of RTE has complained that 'the sociologists have come into the picture a little late in the day . . . the absence of any effective sociological thinking and study about the effects of the new medium has led, in Ireland as elsewhere, to a situation where charges of trivialization, of incitement to violence, of usurpation of authority and of commercial exploitation of the public are levelled against television'. RTE is now sponsoring a project to assess the social effects of television which is being executed by the Centre for Mass Communication Research, University of Leicester. The Director-General feels, however, that 'information about the effects and implications of new technology will always lag far behind the application of technology unless a research element is built into overall planning at the very outset'.[11]

Third, a concern with advertising as allegedly exercising an undue influence on programming. The severest attack on advertising has been directed at radio and television advertising. There is a viewpoint that much contemporary advertising is unethical, immoral and socially undesirable and it has been asserted that programme-makers are influenced by TAM ratings and hence by commercial considerations. On the other hand it has been argued that, as advertising provides a level of revenue which licence revenue or copy sales cannot effect alone and which the media cannot economically forego, then, in so far as it rescues the media from dependence on the State, it assists their independence and thus the democratic process. Moreover very little is known about the social impact of advertising; Irish advertisers express 'general satisfaction with media research but strong criticisms of the lack of advertising effectiveness research'.[12] Once again the data necessary for a truly constructive argument and policy basis is missing.

6.5 Research

It would appear then that there is a widespread awareness of the value of social participation in the operation of the mass media. In the absence of native communication research, however, debate in this area—as indeed in the area of communication professions—on priorities, and ways and means of achieving them, must rely heavily on transposing, in a most general fashion, the conclusions of research elsewhere and on *a priori* intellectual assumptions. This is clearly unsatisfactory; there is a major need for systematic communications studies whose findings might guide future discussions and actions in Ireland.

REFERENCES

1. Denis McQuail, op. cit., p. 58.
2. *The Restoration of the Irish Language: Progress Report for the Period ended 31 March, 1966,* p. 28, Dublin, Stationery Office, 1966.
3. 'A View of Irish Broadcasting', op. cit.
4. *The Devlin Report,* p. 182, 188, 189.
5. Justin Keating, in *Modern Communications and Community Development,* op. cit., p. 36.
6. Brian Farrell, in Keating, op. cit., p. 17.
7. John Fanning, 'RTE Feedback', *Leargas/Public Affairs,* Vol. 4, No. 7, March 1972, p. 3.
8. Committee on Industrial Progress, op. cit., p. 107.
9. Diarmuid O'Broin, in *Management,* Vol. 18, No. 3, March 1971, p. 36.
10. Brochure of the Catholic Communications Institute of Ireland.
11. T. P. Hardiman, quoted in *Irish Times,* 21 November 1972.
12. Dr A. C. Cunningham, in reference to John A. Murphy, 'Irish Advertising Agencies as seen by their Clients', *Management,* Vol. 17, No. 5, May 1970, p. 49-53.

7 Conclusions and trends

Mass communications media are uniquely a feature of modern society; 'it now makes sense to regard a moderate degree of exposure to mass media as at least a mark and possibly even a requirement of modern society'.[1] In Ireland the advent of television alone has been the occasion of 'a major change in social behaviour . . . today only work and sleep take up more of the day than watching television'.[2] The conduct of the mass media is then a matter of central importance, and the response that this calls forth in terms of formal measures, attitudes and assumptions may be said to constitute, more or less explicitly, a communications policy.

Since 1958 economic planning has been an accepted feature of public policy in Ireland; the scope of the Third Programme (1969-72) was extended to 'Economic and Social Development'. Social development aims were concentrated naturally in such basic areas as health, education, housing and income maintenance; but the programme did have incidental reference to fostering cultural and artistic values, the preservation and development of our national heritage and provision for the better use of leisure.

Something is already being done in this area in so far as it relates to the mass media. A civics syllabus introduced into post-primary schools in 1966 drew attention to the role of the mass media as sources of information and entertainment and as potential agents in the integration of an international community. In addition the Department of Education has established an audio-visual aids unit to promote the use of such aids in Irish schools. More generally the Parliamentary Secretary to the Minister for Education now discharges certain responsibilities in respect of 'education for leisure'; if at present policy 'tends to concentrate on physical recreation . . . and sport . . . as leisure forms'[3] it clearly allows of more general development.

Mass communications media are increasingly being utilized in the execution of public policy. RTE and the Department of Education co-operate in the provision of educational broadcasts to schools. Radio na Gaeltachta has been established to 'reflect the unique tradition and genius of the living culture and language of the Gaeltacht',[4] and in support of public policy in respect of the Irish language.

Since the terms of reference of the Broadcasting Review Committee invited 'recommendations considered appropriate in regard to the further development of the services' new initiatives may be expected in this sector. Radio Telefís Éireann's own submission to the Committee requested: (a) a coherent financial plan for broadcasting including a licence fee review body and the transfer to RTE of responsibility for the collection of licence fees; (b) a second radio service on VHF; (c) the development of local radio; (d) the development of full colour television; (e) the provision of a second publicly owned television service of a limited kind; (f) the retention of wired television development as far as possible under the control of the Authority; (g) the setting up of an advisory council on broadcasting; (h) broadcasting access to Oireachtas proceedings; (i) better facilities to improve the reception of RTE radio and television programmes in Northern Ireland and radio programmes in Great Britain.

These developments do not, however, constitute as yet a comprehensive mass communications programme based on estimated needs at local/regional, national and international level, even within the area of public policy. To the extent that public policy largely determines the environment within which policy is formulated on other levels it may be regarded as the critical area. The prospect of more elaborate 'communication planning' in the public sector is greatly dependent on the level of social and political understanding such a policy would be likely to command. While planning now commands a wide degree of acceptance in Irish society, public approval of its extension to the sensitive area of mass communication policy might pose major problems.

Nevertheless, the Devlin report expressed the view that '. . . the role of government in a modern society becomes more and more concerned with the economic, social and cultural development of the people'.[5] This view was the basis of the recommendation that a Department of National Culture be established with responsibility for the Irish language and its associated culture, the national heritage, recreation, and 'the arts and cultural media', including RTE.

An acceptance of this proposal would radically alter the entire context of public policy formation in respect of mass communication media, which must now be accepted as a primary influence on the cultural evolution of modern societies; and, in the case of the publicly owned broadcasting services particularly, the environment within which the media institutions define their own policy.

REFERENCES

1. Denis McQuail, op. cit., p. 3.
1. R. K. Gahan, (Advertisement Sales Controller, RTE), in *Management*, Vol. 17, No. 12, December 1970, p. 23.
3. Robert Molloy, T.D., then Parliamentary Secretary to Minister for Education, in *Management,* Vol. 16, No. 11, November 1969, p. 7.
4. George Colley, T.D., then Minister for Finance and for the Gaeltacht, quoted in *Irish Times,* 21 August 1972.
5. The Devlin report, p. 154.

Appendixes

Socio-economic and cultural background: the Republic of Ireland

Section A : POPULATION

Area: 27,136 square miles; 70,282 square kilometres

Population	1926	1961	1966	1971
(millions):	2.97	2.81	2.88	2.97

Population
density (1971):   110 per square mile;
42 per square kilometre

	1926—46	1946—61	1961—71
Net emigration:	353,870	530,685	141,525

Population-residential pattern, 1966

	%
Dublin area	25.5
Three towns over 30,000	7.4
Towns over 5,000	9.2
Towns over 1,500	7.0
Rural	50.9

Population-age structure, 1966

	%
0-14 years	31.3
15-29 years	20.6
30-44 years	16.1
45-64 years	20.9
65 years and over	11.1
Size of dependent group	42.1

Major religious denominations, 1961

	%
Roman Catholic	94.9
Church of Ireland	3.7
Others	1.4

Number of persons in full-time education, 1970

First level	526,765
Second level	208,547
Third level	26,217[1]

1. As a proportion of 20-24 age group (1968): 10.4 per cent

Size of Gaeltacht (Irish-speaking communities)

1961	1966
73,416	72,706
2.8 per cent	2.5 per cent

In 1961 27 per cent of the population was 'capable of speaking Irish'.

Section B : ECONOMY

GNP at market prices:	1970	1971
(£ million)	1,677	1,968
Income per capita *(£):*	582	660

Average annual rate of growth, 1960–70

Total	Per capita
3.9 per cent	3.5 per cent

Origins of Gross Domestic Product at factor cost (percentages)

Year	Agriculture	Industry	Services/ government
1969	17.8	35.2	47
1971	16.4	35.6	48

Civilian employment by sector of economy (percentages)

Year	Agriculture	Industry	Services/ government
1969	28.4	29.7	41.9
1971	26.5	30.9	42.6

Section C : DEVELOPMENT INDICATORS

Expectation of life at birth (1965–67)	Males	68.6 years
	Females	72.9 years
Animal protein (grammes per inhabitant per day, 1970)		62
Doctors per 100,000, 1969		102
Consumption of electricity (kW per head per year, 1971)		1,786
Telephones (per 1,000 inhabitants, 1970)		104
Passenger cars (per 1,000 inhabitants, 1970)		134
Television sets (per 1,000 inhabitants, 1972)		180
Total public expenditure (capital and current) as percentage of GNP, 1970/71		42

Mass media in the Republic of Ireland

Section A : PAPER, PAPER PRODUCTS, PRINTING AND PUBLISHING, 1969

	Gross output (£ million)	Employment
Total industry (1)	53.5	16,350
of which printing and publishing (2)	29.5	10,710
(2) as percentage of (1)	55	65

Printing and publishing, 1969:

Exports as percentage (by value) of gross output: approx. 9 per cent.
Imports as percentage (by value) of gross output: approx. 20 per cent.

Sources: Irish Statistical Bulletin, December 1972, p. 264, 265; CIP, *Report on Paper, Paper Products, Printing and Publishing Industry,* 1970, Appendix IX, and calculations therefrom.

5*

Section B : NEWSPAPERS, 1969

	Gross output (£ million)	Imports (£ million)	Exports (£ million)
Printing of newspapers	12.34	0.37	1.18
of which			
National newspapers	approx. 75 per cent		
Provincial newspapers	approx. 25 per cent		

Sources: As in Section A, with CIP report, op. cit., p. 95.

Circulation of national newspapers in Ireland

Irish Independent	(1905)	166,697
Irish Press	(1931)	97,047
Irish Times	(1859)	63,128
Cork Examiner	(1841)	61,329
Seven British papers		approx. 53,000
Evening Herald	(1891)	133,088
Evening Press	(1954)	145,273
Evening Echo (Cork)		35,915
Sunday Independent	(1906)	353,237
Sunday Press	(1949)	442,817
Sunday World	(1973)	210,000[1]
Seven British papers		approx. 525,000

1. Initial controlled figure.

Sources: ABC figures for six months ending December 1972, for Irish papers: For British papers, estimate derived from *Newspaper Press Directory 1971-72.*

Circulation of provincial newspapers in Ireland

Under 5,000	1
5,000-10,000	9
10,000-15,000	14
15,000-20,000	8
20,000-25,000	1
25,000-30,000	3[1]
30,000-40,000	—
Over 40,000	1

1. Includes total for People (Wexford) Group (four papers).

Source: derived from *Communications Directory and Yearbook 1973*, Section 3.

Rank order of newspaper customers in terms of revenue

National press	Provincial press
1. Newsagents	Advertising agents
2. Advertising agents	Newsagents
3. Booksellers/stationers	Industrial/commercial offices
4. Industrial/commercial offices	Booksellers/stationers
5. Publishers	Publishers
6. Public service	Public service

Source: CIP report, op. cit., p. 118, table 3.

Content (percentage) of Irish morning daily newspapers, 1967

	Irish Independent	Irish Press	Irish Times	Cork Examiner
Editorial	61	78	70	61
of which News	69	67	70	78
of which				
Political-social-cultural	35	38	41	46
Domestic	23	26	19	28
International	12	12	22	18

Source: Chubb, *The Government and Politics of Ireland*, p. 127–8, tables 5.1, 5.2.

Readership pattern of Irish newspapers (15 years +) (percentages)

	All	Urban	Rural
Morning	59	63	54
Evening	45	68	21
Sunday	81	80	82
Provincial	59	39	80

Age	15-24	25-34	35-44	45-54	55-64	65+
Morning	59	61	61	64	57	49
Evening	51	54	46	44	42	32
Sunday	84	81	83	86	80	70
Provincial	60	55	60	62	58	57

	AB	C1	C2	DE	F1	F2
Morning	86	80	65	50	61	36
Evening	58	60	65	55	17	13
Sunday	83	83	86	76	85	76
Provincial	36	52	52	49	86	72

AB: Upper middle/middle class.
C1: Lower middle class.
C2: Skilled manual workers.
DE: Semi-skilled/unskilled workers.
F1: Farmers with holdings over 30 acres.
F2: Farmers with holdings under 30 acres.

Source: National Readership Survey, 1968, tables 1A and 1B.

67

5

Section C : PUBLISHING, 1969

(Precise figures for the publishing sectors are difficult to obtain; however, the following table may give some general indication of the scope of the sectors.)

	Gross output (£ million)	Exports (£ million)	Imports (£ million)
Books	2.82	0.27	1.79
Periodicals	0.99	0.13	1.20
Other (except newspapers)[1]	8.87	1.73	1.79
	12.68	2.13	4.78

1. 'Other' includes picture postcards, calendars, tickets, etc.

Source: Derived from *Irish Statistical Bulletin,* December 1972, and CIP report (1970), op. cit.

Books and pamphlets

In 1969 a total of 992 recorded titles were issued by 209 recorded publishers (both figures inclusive of Northern Ireland).
As indicated in the text at paragraph 4.2.1, many such 'publishers' issue only a single title. In 1968 for instance only eleven publishers issued more than ten titles and together these publishers accounted for over 60 per cent of titles issued that year.

Analysis of 1969 domestic titles by area of interest

Category	Number of titles
Bibliography and general	24
Philosophy and psychology	10
Religion and theology	49
Social science and government	349
School textbooks	51
Language and philology	7
Pure sciences	16
Technology, medicine, business	82
Music, art, recreation	65
Literature and criticism	131
History, biography, geography	165
New serial titles	43

These figures need to be assessed with caution; titles listed range from individual volumes of the 1,000-volume production of British Parliamentary papers to polemical pamphlets.

Source: Irish Publishing Record 1969, p. 1.

The report of the Committee on Industrial Progress (1970) recorded that 'no reliable statistics are available showing the size or extent of the market for books in Ireland' (p. 141). However, John M. Feehan, in *An Irish Publisher and his World* (Mercier, 1969, p. 84), has suggested that a successful paperback might sell up to 15,000 copies on the domestic market.

Periodicals: analysis of 1972 domestic periodical production by area of interest

Trade, technical, professional	70
Religion	55
Agriculture	37
Education	30
Sport, leisure	28
Medicine	20
Learning, culture	19
Business, public affairs	16
Politics	14
Irish language	12
Woman and youth sector	9

Source: *Communication Directory and Yearbook 1973*, Section 4.

Domestic periodicals with circulation in excess of 100,000

Title	Published	Interest	Approximate circulation
Golden Pages	(1969) Yearly	Telephone directory	380,000
The Far East	(1918) Monthly	Missionary activity	205,000
Africa	(1931) Monthly	Missionary activity	160,000
Dublin Post	(1970) Weekly	City news/advertising	120,000

Sources: *Communication Directory and Yearbook 1973*, Section 3; *Newspaper Press Directory 1972–72*, p. 11.

Circulation of weekly periodicals included in 1968 readership survey

Title	Interest	Circulation
Womans Way (1963)	per title	90,000
RTE Guide (1961)	per title	85,211
Irish Farmers' Journal (1948)	per title	67,140
Irish Catholic (1888)	per title	49,166
Ireland's Own (1902)	Rural Ireland	45,504
Catholic Standard (1938)	per title	23,850

Sources: Titles—*National Readership Survey, 1968*; circulation—*Newspaper Press Directory 1971-72*, p. 11.

Section D : LIBRARIES (Book volumes, in thousands) 1968

National Library	17,500[1]
Four university libraries	621
Three specialized libraries	268
Thirty-one public libraries with 3,836 service points	3,300

1. Metres of occupied shelves.
Source: Unesco Statistical Yearbook 1970, table 4.1.

Public libraries

	1961—62	1972—73
Revenue expenditure (£ million)	0.43	1.34[1]
Book volumes (millions)	2.51	4.09
Book issues (millions)	10.73	18.44
Registered borrowers		
Adults	244,829	286,395
Children	138,603	293,863
TOTAL	383,752	580,258

1. Estimate.
Source: 24th Annual Report of An Chomhairle Leabharlann, 31 March 1972.

Section E : CINEMA

Cinema and theatre establishments

Year	Total no.		No. in census	Paid admissions	Visits per capita	Gross receipts (£ million)	Full-time employment
1956	341		286	52.1	18	5.01	2,630
1966	267		196	21.9	8	4.92	2,378
			%	%		%	
1966		Dublin area	78	40		60	
		Three other cities	17	50		13	
		All other	5	10		27	

Sources: Statistical Abstract (1962), table 158; *Census of Distribution and Services: Wholesale Trade and Services (1966),* table 60, with calculations therefrom.

Cinema audiences (percentages), 1968 (15 years +)

Went to a cinema:

	All	Urban	Rural
Yesterday	3	4	1
2 to 28 days ago	27	36	17
Longer ago/never	71	60	82

	Age 15-24	25-34	35-44	45-54	55-64	65 +
Yesterday	6	3	2	1	1	0
2 to 28 days ago	56	40	22	15	12	3
Longer ago/never	37	57	76	84	88	96

	AB	C1	C2	DE	F1	F2
Yesterday	2	5	4	3	1	0
2 to 28 days ago	42	36	34	27	18	14
Longer ago/never	56	59	63	70	71	86

AB: Farmers with holdings under 30 acres.
C1: Lower middle class.
C2: Skilled manual workers.
DE: Semi-skilled/unskilled workers.
F1: Farmers with holdings over 30 acres.
F2: Upper middle/middle class.

Source: National Readership Survey, 1968, table SC.

Section F : RADIO AND TELEVISION

Year	Medium	Income (£ million)	Expenditure (£ million)
1961/62	Radio	0.663	0.644
	Television	0.463	0.453
	TOTAL	1.126	1.097
1971/72	Radio	1.480	2.181
	Television	5.526	4.816
	TOTAL	7.006	6.997

Source of income 1971/72 (percentages)

Radio advertising	10.5 ⎞	
Television advertising	41.5 ⎠	52
Radio-licence fees	10.0 ⎞	
Television-licence fees	35.0 ⎠	45
Other		3
		100

Hours of broadcasting, 1971/72

Radio : 5,767   Television : 2,420
                       Home-originated: 1,041
                                  Imported: 1,379

	%		%	Light entertain-	%
Music	31	News	22	ment	27
Talks/features	19.5	Sports	18	Adventure/fiction	26
News	15	Public affairs	16	Children's	16
		Light entertain-			
Plays/variety	12	ment	12	Drama	12
Sponsored	11	Schools	8	Public affairs	7

Sources: RTE Annual Report 1971–72.

Radio coverage

	%
Individuals	99
Households	91
Households with more than one set	18
Households with portable sets	56
Households with VHF	16
Households with car radios	5

In May 1972, 60 per cent of the adult population listened to radio sometime
each day; 66 per cent of these (46 per cent of all adults) listened to RTE.

Source: Audience listenership survey, RTE, May 1972.

Television viewed yesterday, 1968 (15 years +) (percentages)[1]

	All	Urban	Rural
RTE	58	67	48
BBC 1	12	16	7
BBC 2	1	1	0
ITV Ulster	8	9	6
ITV Wales	5	9	1

Age	15-24	25-34	35-44	45-54	55-64	65 +
RTE	64	62	63	58	53	45
BBC 1	14	13	11	13	12	9
BBC 2	1	1	0	0	1	0
ITV Ulster	8	9	7	7	8	7
ITV Wales	6	8	7	6	4	3

1. These figures are rather dated. In 1968 only 72 per cent of individuals in
64 per cent of households were receiving television as compared to 84 per cent
of individuals in 78 per cent of households in 1973. Multi-channel television
homes as a proportion of all television homes were 36 per cent in 1968 and 37 per
cent in 1972.

	AB	C1	C2	DE	F1	F2
RTE	56	71	69	61	52	35
BBC 1	19	15	16	12	7	6
BBC 2	1	0	1	1	0	0
ITV Ulster	10	8	9	9	5	5
ITV Wales	7	8	9	6	1	1

AB: Upper middle/middle class.
C1: Lower middle class.
C2: Skilled manual workers.
DE: Semi-skilled/unskilled workers.
F1: Farmers with holdings over 30 acres.
F2: Farmers with holdings under 30 acres.

Source: National Readership Survey, 1968, tables 1A, 1B.

Employment

In 1971/72 RTE had 1,520 full-time employees.

Gross amounts charged to clients by Irish advertising agencies[1]

	1961 (£ million)	1971 (£ million)
Press	2.41	5.85
Bill-posting/Transport advertising	0.10	0.30
Radio	0.13	0.87
Television	0.05	3.69
Film screen time	0.05	0.11
Printing	0.15	0.73
Other	0.06	1.29
TOTAL	2.95	12.84

Source: Communications Directory and Yearbook, 1973, p. 144.

1. On the basis of 1968 data, advertising agencies are estimated to handle 75 per cent of total advertising expenditure (cf. *Management,* Vol. XVI, No. 3, March 1969, p. 29, 33).

Employment in advertising agencies, 1971

Self-employed	100
Full-time employees	875
TOTAL	975

Source: Communications Directory and Yearbook, 1973.